Measure Twice,
Cut Once

Measure Twice, Cut Once

LESSONS FROM A
MASTER CARPENTER

Norm Abram

LITTLE, BROWN AND COMPANY
Boston New York London

First Edition

Library of Congress Cataloging-in-Publication Data

Abram, Norm.
    Measure twice, cut once : lessons from a master carpenter / Norm
Abram. — 1st ed.
        p.   cm.
    ISBN 0-316-00494-4
    1. Woodwork. 2. Carpentry. 1. Title.
    TT185.A26   1996
684 — dc20   96-7584
                                                                   CIP

10   9   8   7

MV-NY

Printed in the United States of America

In memory of Louis L. Abram, 1925–1995

CONTENTS

[viii]

[ix]

Measure Twice,
Cut Once

Family Album

AMONG THE SNAPSHOTS my parents kept of my childhood, there are two in which I'm wearing the same snowsuit and smiling cheerfully. (I'd guess I was three or four years old.) The photographs are like alternate destinies. The earlier of the pictures, judging from how old I look, was probably taken in late fall. It must have been cold enough to warrant a snowsuit, but there is no snow on the ground. I'm poised to push a wheelbarrow that my father made from spare pieces of wood and metal strapping. His shadow stretching across the foreground grass identifies the photographer. The wheelbarrow looks startlingly like one I built for a television woodworking project a few years ago.

In the twin photograph, I'm standing in front of a spruce tree laden with snow. Winter boots and a scarf have been added to my outfit. I'm holding a hockey stick as though poised to flash across a rink. A carpenter or an aspiring Bobby Orr — that seems to be the question posed by the snapshots. My father certainly left career decisions entirely in my hands and never pushed me to learn his trade. But although I've always loved both winter and summer sports, there was never much question about my desire to emulate my father's skills.

This little book describes some of the things I've learned in approximately thirty years of serious carpentry. As you will see, a carpenter is a blend of what he learns from his mentors and what he makes of his trade over time. Every experienced carpenter has his own "take" on tools and techniques, his idiosyncrasies that he passes on to others. Even though many of my contemporaries consider me a champion of power tools, most of what I have to say here concerns work with hand tools. They largely defined my father's career, and mastering them is how I began. If I had to execute a complicated piece of carpentry today at a job site without electricity or gas, I'd proceed as confidently as if I had my circular saw and pneumatic hammer.

My father once built a lakeside cottage, which is still in the family. He even dug the well for the cottage by hand; its cover has the date inscribed, a month before I was born. Relatives of my mother's owned land nearby. They operated small truck farms and lakeside picnic areas in addition to pursuing their regular jobs. As a youngster, I earned spending money policing the picnic areas and working in their gardens. My first driving experience was on a tractor at one of these farms.

Since my father worked on the cottage only in his spare time, construction stretched out over a period of months. He didn't confine himself to its carpentry — to framing, roofing, siding, and interior finish work. He also laid the stone foundation as well as the brick chimney. A few years ago, he and I did some renovation of the cottage. In rebuilding the gutters, which had deteriorated over time, we used a power miter box to streamline the cutting. But my dad did all the original gutter and trim work with hand tools.

Another family photograph shows me as a toddler standing next to some large rocks behind the cottage. The cottage itself looks complete except for the missing steps from the back porch to the lawn. I'm holding a sledgehammer larger than I am, pretending I have enough strength to break the rocks into stones for the steps.

In the same period, my father built a trailer to haul behind our car. He assembled an old car axle and bits of pipe and steel and welded them together into a frame. The bed of the trailer was made by attaching planks to the frame with machine screws driven into holes that had been tapped into the steel. Again, there is a black-and-white photograph of me trying to use a screwdriver to help attach the planks. The screwdriver was almost as large as I was! If some carpenters are indeed born, not made, I guess I belong to the genetic fraternity. Truly, there are aspects of working with tools that I sense are in my blood.

Handy Andy

A YEAR OR so after my father began the lakeside cottage, he also started to build the house I grew up in. This house, too, took shape at the pace that my father's free time permitted. I remember, for example, that felt paper secured with wooden battens *was* the siding for a long time, until he could proceed to the finish exterior of brick. What made the deepest impression on me was my father's self-reliance. When we needed a house, he built it. When the car needed to be repaired or the washing machine broke down or a pipe leaked, he fixed it.

I was about seven when I got my first toolbox for Christmas, a metal box called a Handy Andy. Inside were a hammer, a saw, a chisel, a block plane, a square, pliers, a screwdriver, and some kind of measuring tape. My recollection is that these tools were designed to enable me to do simple carpentry, yet were safe enough to minimize the chance of injury. I'm sure I was pleased to have the tools. I don't recall being disappointed in their quality, but I was by that age already familiar with hand tools designed for adult work.

When I was nine, my father took me to work on a job with him for the first time. (A year before, he had left the woolen mill where he had maintained and repaired machines and buildings to take up carpentry full-time.) I can't recall why he took me that day rather than another, but I remember that he was laying a hardwood floor. And I remember the date — Christmas Eve. On the way home that night, when my dad asked what I wanted for Christmas, I said I hoped to get a bicycle. The next day I received my first bicycle, a 26-inch Schwinn Corvette (the top of the line in those days). It was a snowless Christmas, and I spent the whole afternoon riding my bike around the lawn.

My father set up a small workshop for himself in the basement of our house. It was very simple compared to the one I have, but it filled his needs. He would sometimes bring home material for cabinets or drawers for a job he was working on. From age eleven or twelve I had my own workbench with a light over it near his. I can't begin to guess how many hours I spent there.

Near my workbench I built a playhouse for my younger sister. Made mostly of strapping (1-by-3-inch spruce or pine) and other surplus wood from my father's work, the playhouse at first had four walls, with openings for a door and windows. Eventually I put a roof on it.

I also had a small flatbed trailer my father had welded together so I could tow light loads behind a pedal-powered tractor. I closed the trailer in with sides and a roof so that it looked something like a miniature horse trailer. When my father took these structures apart years later, he told my mother they had an awful lot of nails in them.

Hydro toys, battery-powered toys, and kits also kept me occupied for hours at a time. I was passionately interested in cars as a youngster and built countless models at my workbench. The motor, gears, and pulleys from my Erector set turned into a saw to cut plastic for the models. I filed a gear into a saw blade and then powered it with the pulleys coupled to the motor with string or rubber bands. Years later, my friends and I would occasionally acquire a wreck of a car and take it apart just to see how it worked. Sometimes the car would run when we put it back together, sometimes not.

Wages

PEOPLE OFTEN ASK me where I went to school to learn carpentry. I absorbed all I know from watching my dad in his basement workshop or by observing him and others on a job and then trying the techniques myself. Or just by experimenting. I still do that. I play around in the workshop, letting intuition and curiosity lead me where they will. My dad never sat me down and said, "This is how to use a screwdriver." He never lectured. I was never pressured to acquire any carpentry skills.

My introduction to work for hire was gradual, beginning with the summer work for my mother's relatives. By age fifteen I was hired by the same contractor for whom my father worked. I didn't work for hire on weekends, nor, as I recall, did my father. But every vacation, long or short, was an opportunity to do some carpentry and earn some money. This contractor undertook small remodeling jobs or additions to houses, projects that required at most two- or three-man crews. At first I was more of a laborer, doing demolition and digging holes, than I was a carpenter's helper, but it wasn't long before I had my first experiences rough framing and using a serious power tool, the circular saw.

Within a few years, when my dad joined a general contracting firm that did new construction, I began to participate in the whole process of building houses. We began our work at a site when the foundation was in place. We framed the structure, installed the roof, trimmed and sided the wood exterior, hung the rock lathe, and did the finish carpentry (doors, windows, closets, cabinetry, stairs, moldings, baseboards, floors, etc.). All the houses were finished with two-coat plaster. We did everything except lay the foundations, plaster, and paint.

There were usually four or five carpenters in the group my father supervised. Some of them were older than he, but none was superior in skill. I think some of them may have resented having a teenager in the group, and the foreman's son at that. Yet my father was scrupulous about not showing me any favoritism. If anything, he leaned in the other direction, giving me the more menial work to do.

In fact, that wasn't bad for me at all. I learned the discipline of carpentry and of work in general. I learned to take pride in doing routine things well. The only person younger than I on any of the jobs was the owner's son. Most of the time I worked on the same site as my father, but not necessarily beside him. The boss occasionally said to my father, "Let's send Norm over to another job site to put down the underlayment for the carpet." These were my first solo professional projects.

Toolboxes

WORKING WITH MY father, I didn't have a toolbox of my own at first. He had plenty of tools, and I borrowed what I needed. Leather toolbelts hadn't yet come into fashion; when they did, I was an early convert. My dad never wore a toolbelt. He wore bibbed overalls with loops and pockets for various hand tools sewn on to them. He wore them over his work clothes all year, even, to my astonishment, in the worst heat of summer. I wore a cloth nail apron and carried the tools I needed at the moment until I graduated to my own toolbox and leather toolbelt.

There are several kinds of toolboxes, each with advantages and disadvantages. Some carpenters carry triangular wood boxes with pole handles but no covers. These days, I often see carpenters lugging around five-gallon drywall compound buckets with drop-in dividers with slots for tools. They're not very elegant, but every tool is visible and easily reached. There is also no stacking, which leads to pawing through layers to uncover the desired tool.

My dad carried a metal carpenter's box with square corners. Its hinged cover swung open to reveal a shallow removable tray sitting over a larger storage compartment. His toolbox was long enough that a 28-inch level could be stored on the underside of the cover. A level is delicate and doesn't benefit from being stacked with other tools inside the box. The level fit over two blocks of wood that were secured to the cover with screws; it was then held firmly in place with homemade metal clips. The tray had limited space for smaller items, such as nail sets, a chalk line, pencils and other marking tools, a plumb bob, and drill bits, which we put in an old metal bandage container.

There weren't any compartments in the space underneath the tray when my father bought the box. He lined the bottom with plywood and then divided the space lengthwise with a wood partition about ½ inch wide and 3 inches high. The narrower side of the space (about a third of the overall width) was just wide enough to hold up to four basic handsaws standing on edge, their handles alternated at each end. There was room to drop a hacksaw, a hatchet, and a combination square in between the standing blades. The remainder of the tools were arranged to his satisfaction in the wider compartment. My father kept a very well organized box.

When I went to work for the Great Eastern Building Company, shortly after college, the boss gave me the tool list he routinely gave each of his carpenters, who were expected to own and carry the full inventory. I already owned every tool on the list — and quite a few others. I set up my own metal toolbox very much as my father had arranged his. I kept my bars in the middle of the larger compartment and my planes at one end. The stacked tools had to include a Yankee screwdriver, a 50-foot tape, and a 100-foot tape.

To protect my chisels from chipped cutting edges, my mother made me the same kind of storage pouch she had made for my father, adapting a method long used for silverware. She took a rectangular piece of heavy canvas, sewed opposing cloth pockets onto one side, and attached two heavy strings to the middle of one of the short ends. I slid my chisels into the pockets as you would slide knives or spoons into pockets of softer material, folded the long edges over so the chisels couldn't fall out, rolled the pouch up, and tied the strings around it. In time, the sharp edges of the chisels cut right through the cloth, but having them in a cloth bundle was much better than their rolling loose in the toolbox.

Toolboxes get very heavy when they're fully loaded.

The kind my dad and I used have handles on the ends as well as on top to make them easier to carry. Some boxes have a slot in the top so that a carpenter can put one leg of a framing square inside and have the other leg project out through the slot. I have always treated my framing square as a loose tool, to be carried outside the toolbox.

A metal toolbox takes a lot of punishment, especially if you transport it, as I did mine for many years, in an open truck bed, where it slides around. Eventually, the bottom rusts out from exposure to moisture. But the species is hardy. I've worn out only two of them. The main advantage of the rectangular metal box is its cover. When you're working outside in damp weather, the protective cover will extend the life of the tools appreciably.

In my years as a professional carpenter and contractor, I always carried both a carpenter's box, with tools mainly for wood construction, and a mechanic's box, with tools for metalwork, tool repair, and truck repair. Often it was sufficient to carry only my carpenter's box to a job site, but I would add a few hand tools — an adjustable wrench and a pair of pliers among them — from my mechanic's box. I never kept a duplicate set of tools. I borrowed the tools I needed from one box to the other, then returned them at job's end.

The Right Way

I SAW A funny movie recently about a carpenter and his three sons. The father, who had just died, spoke some of his best lines from his coffin. For instance: "There's only two ways to do things. There's the right way, and there's my way. And they're the same way!" The line reminded me of my somewhat autocratic grandfather. He was a supervisor in a woolen mill, but he knew carpentry and performed it well. In his generation, the family was large and close, but my grandfather was boss and no one dared disagree with him. My dad, on the other hand, never said or implied that his way was the right way. But since he hadn't come from a tradition of open discussion, he and I didn't talk about carpentry as much, looking back, as I wish we had.

When I started building my own house about five years ago, my dad had already been retired for a number of years. It didn't seem possible, given the demands of my other work, that I could do nearly as much of the construction myself as my father had done of his house. There were many tasks that I keenly wanted to do but had to consign to others in the interest of getting the house ready for occupancy in a reasonable period of time. But some jobs I did save for myself, for the satisfaction of working on the house of my dreams.

I didn't anticipate that my father would get involved, but he volunteered to do certain tasks, and I saw that he was enjoying it. He hadn't kept up with the development of tools during his retirement, and I think he was shocked by some of the changes. Nevertheless he adapted quickly. After I showed him how to use my power tools, I soon saw him working as comfortably as though he had been using them all his life. He seemed content, for example, to switch over from nailing by hand to using a pneumatic nailer. What shocked me in turn was the change in our relationship. He began each of his visits by asking me what I wanted him to do. His request for direction caught me off-guard. I was used to hearing *him* say: "Do this." "Take care of that."

The contents of the toolbox my father carried to my new house were quite different from mine. Though he hadn't used one for a number of years, for instance, my dad still carried a bit brace and a set of bits. He had his ripsaws in addition to crosscut saws. Our pry bars were different. I don't know whether a Cat's Paw was even available when my father started to build the lakeside cottage forty-five years ago, but

I know the design of the flat bar has evolved significantly in my lifetime.

In my generation, technology has changed many hand tools and introduced the power tools that have largely superseded some of them. Yet many aspects of carpentry are very much as they were in my father's day or in my grandfather's. Even if the tool has evolved, the method is the same. There are many situations in which nothing works as well as a hammer and a chisel. I can't imagine technology reaching the point where there would be no need for the deceptively simple technique of scribing.

What has declined from my dad's generation to mine is the prevailing standard of skill in carpentry. My father could do many things by hand that I've never practiced enough to do, such as ripping a long board by hand in an admirably straight line. Recently I helped to renovate an old house in Salem, Massachusetts. A number of handsome frame houses in Salem's historic district have overlapping clapboards on their sides and backs; the facades, however, are made of very long boards butted square against each other to make a flat surface. An overlapping clapboard can be less than perfectly straight, but there can't be much divergence when the boards are butted. In Salem, many facades reveal an excellent fit everywhere in long boards sawn and planed two centuries ago — by hand.

Carpentry was once a classic trade in the sense that techniques were treated as secrets to be revealed only to the chosen few, handed down from one generation to the next. Much of my time during the past two decades has been spent demystifying the skills of carpentry and woodworking so that any interested person can acquire the tools, learn the techniques, and practice them to an aspired level of skill. Hence this book. It will discuss the contents of the ideal toolbox of today, not the tools that sufficed for my father's superior carpentry. But as I describe hand tools and offer tips on techniques I've adopted, I never forget that much of what I know and practice was handed down to me from my dad and others of his and earlier generations. I hope these lessons will give you the confidence to use more tools, to augment your toolbox and workshop, and to share your experience and wisdom with others.

Measure Twice, Cut Once, but Don't Measure at All if You Can Avoid It

NEVER MEASURE UNLESS you have no choice. Instead, base your marking and cutting on the actual situation. For example, I would never measure an exterior wall for a piece of siding, then go off and measure a length, cut it, and bring it back to install. It doesn't matter how long the siding needs to be: I hold a length up where I intend to install it and mark it in place for cutting. It's the actual length that's important, not the numerical symbols on my tape measure.

Tape measures vary. The longer they're used, the more they stretch. The hook at the end gets gummed up or bent enough to cause slight variations in readings. I don't assume that my own tape is perfect. If I'm working alone, I know that all the measurements are taken from my own tape and therefore provide uniform variations from a true standard. But if I'm working with other carpenters and each of us uses his own tape, with its unique variation from true, the consequences take on real importance. I've often seen carpenters argue at a lumber pile about whether a piece was cut to the right length, only to find that their tapes were not equal.

I can take three tape measures, even made by the same manufacturer, from three different carpenters and lay them out for comparison; each will differ slightly from the others. When very precise work is called for, it is best to use the same measuring tool throughout the job. Switching from one rule or tape to another can cause variations, and you will have a hard time detecting how and where the measurements went astray.

If one of your projects involves repeating the same measurement accurately time after time — for example, when installing courses of shingles on a roof or a side wall — use cumulative measurements rather than individual markings.

Aldren Watson, in his excellent guidebook, *Hand Tools: Their Ways and Workings*, spins another sage variation on our aphorism: "While 'measure twice and cut once' is always pithy advice, it is more important to measure *accurately* and to know that you have."

House Rules

EARLY IN MY career, I used a wooden folding rule for all measurements except for layout in framing, when I used 50- or 100-foot steel tapes. In recent years I haven't carried a wooden rule in my toolbox, and I rarely see other carpenters use one. But now I have second thoughts, because there are many situations in which it is the ideal tool. I'll never find a steel tape that I can extend between two walls, or use for other inside measurements, and get as accurate a reading as I can with a folding rule. A folding rule, moreover, is a good substitute for a square when scribing a line on a board to follow when ripping the board to width. It is as easy to carry as a steel tape, since both fit easily into a pocket.

The best folding rules are made of hardwood with brass fittings; their riveted swivel joints lock automatically to minimize inaccuracies due to an arm's being slightly bent. Gradations should be marked on both sides in sixteenths and embedded in the wood so that they remain legible, even after long use. Folding rules range from 6 to 8 feet, but I think a 6-footer is the most desirable for general carpentry. There is a certain frailty about this tool. It is easily damaged if anyone steps on a joint when the rule is opened out. A falling hammer or other heavy object can shatter an open wooden arm. Fold up the rule promptly after a measurement rather than leaving it with open arms.

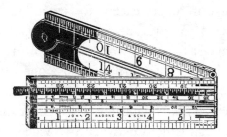

Antique folding wooden rule with sliding brass extension

If the joints of a folding rule get too stiff, a few drops of machine oil will quickly make them pliable again. The opposite problem is more common: the joints may become too loose after extensive use. In this case, unfortunately, not much can be done.

A new folding rule is apt to be uncomfortably stiff. After a certain amount of use, it gets broken in and works easily — indeed, beautifully. I like to watch an expert tradesman flip a rule open, take a measurement or two, and fold it up almost faster than the eye can follow, the joints opening and closing so quickly that they clatter like castanets — carpentry at its most graceful.

An extension rule is a folding rule with a slender sliding brass arm set in a groove in the end arm. The brass arm can be extended several inches to give the tool the flexibility its rigid arms otherwise lack for inside measurements; it is essential to a good rule. My father always insisted on searching for double-extension rules, with brass bars on both ends. He said the time spent looking for this less common style was quickly made up in time saved on the job, since he never had to look for the end with the brass arm.

Blades

As I MENTIONED earlier, I used a 50-foot metal tape for framing layout when I was still using a wooden folding rule for other measurements. Both 50- and 100-foot tapes became common for laying out foundations when most carpenters were still using wooden rules for all their other measurements. Surveyors also used the long metal tapes. It was the introduction of metal tapes with 16-, 20-, and

25-foot blades that drove wooden rules to the brink of extinction. Most of the 16- and 20-foot tapes have ¾-inch-wide blades. Twenty-five-foot tapes may have 1-inch-wide blades.

Pocket tape

I personally don't like inch-wide blades. The blade of my favorite steel tape is ¾ inch wide and 20 feet long. There's no mystery about this. The longest lumber I use with any frequency is 16 feet long. For the bulk of my work, I handle boards and sheets that range from 6 to 12 feet long and a few inches to 4 feet wide. If you could examine a 20-foot tape I used for a year or two, you would see unmistakable signs of wear over the first 12 feet of the blade; the remainder would look almost new.

Earlier this year I tried using an inexpensive metal tape. Within two weeks the blade split. Save yourself some grief and buy well-made tapes and rules. A tape should last at least two years, even with heavy use. What I've found chews up tapes quickly is framing, where they're always getting stepped on or abused in some other way. I want a tape to be as light as possible (consistent with quality) because — clipped to my belt or in my pocket — I'll be carrying it all day.

The blade of a metal tape is slightly concave, to improve its rigidity when extended. Your markings will be more accurate if you roll the blade slightly so that one of the edges touches the surface you are measuring. Likewise, when you are using a wooden rule, it is best to turn the arms up on one edge so that the gradations are right next to the marking surface rather than placing the rule flat and looking down on it; you're liable to be looking down at an angle rather than straight down, and that can throw your marking off.

A "helpful hint" I read recently suggested that you practice reading measurements upside down, to help in situations when the rule or tape is upside down and it would be annoying to have to reverse it. The hint reminded me of some nosy reporters who've confessed that they practiced reading upside down so they could interview someone and at the same time read anything on the person's desk. That kind of mischief might take some practice. But it doesn't take much practice to read a measuring tool accurately upside down, and fairly regularly I do.

Several weeks ago I looked through a catalogue of well-made tools. The measuring tools section included a 25-foot tape with a "very rugged" case. Its special feature was a battery-powered liquid crystal display on the top that indicated digitally in either inches (to 1/16) or centimeters (to 1 mm) the exact distance the tape had been pulled out or the distance, including the case, for inside measurements. There was even a memory button that could preserve the last reading, even after the blade was returned to the case. The perpetual variations on basic tools astonish me. Here, however, I dislike the 1-inch width of the blade, and I haven't experienced trouble (yet) reading the blade itself or remembering a measurement I've just made. I turned the page.

Over the Long Stretch

FIFTY- AND 100-FOOT tapes are not curved cross-wise for rigidity like shorter metal tapes. They are flat and narrower, the blade only 3/8 inch wide compared to the 3/4 or full inch of the shorter tapes. The narrowness makes them lighter, easier to pull taut at the distances for which they're designed. They are usually calibrated to 1/8 inch because they are used for measurements that don't require the refinement of ⅟₁₆ or more.

100-foot steel rule

The hook on a 25-foot tape is simply a piece of metal attached at a right angle to the end of the tape so that you can catch it on one end of a piece of material as you pull the tape out. On longer tapes, the end is a loop with a hook that folds out to 90 degrees to catch on whatever you're measuring; the loop and hook device takes up a little more than the first inch. Either type of end — the plain catch or the combination loop and catch — can get damaged in use and cause inaccuracies if measurements include the very end of the tape. Whenever precision is called for, I begin measurements with my 20-foot tape on its 1-inch mark and with my 50- and 100-foot tapes on their 2-inch marks. It is a good safeguard against distortion at the end of the tape as long as you discipline yourself not to forget to allow for the amount you have shortened the tape. (If you're laying out a known measurement, add the inches;

if you're measuring an unknown distance, subtract the inches.)

Knowing that many tapes are going to be used frequently for layouts of studs, joists, or rafters 16 inches on center, manufacturers make them with the 16-inch intervals highlighted by numerals in a different color. When you're laying out 2-by-4-inch studs, for example, that will be faced with 4-by-8-foot sheets of plywood or drywall, you want the end of a sheet to fall on the center of a stud, where it can butt against the next sheet. If you put your tape at the left end of a wall you're laying out, mark out 16-inch intervals to the right, and place the studs to the right of each mark, you will find that the end of an 8-foot sheet will not fall, as you hoped, in the center of the seventh stud; it will fall short. But if you cut a ¾-inch scrap block (half the thickness of a stud, since a typical 2-by stud is 1½ inches thick), place it as an extension on the left side where the measurement begins, and anchor your tape to include the extra block, the first sheet will end at the center of the seventh stud; the rest of the sheets will also fall at the center of studs.

This layout method saves material because any starter piece cut is a multiple of 16 inches and will fall on the center of a framing member, and waste material will fit without additional cutting because it, too, will be a multiple of 16 inches.

Metal tapes of all lengths are affected by wet weather. A damp tape attracts sawdust, dirt, or other small bits of debris and carries some of it back into the case when retracted. If you don't guard against the accumulation of unwanted material inside the case, it will eventually be difficult, maybe impossible, to retract the tape fully. At the end of a damp day, I fully extend any tapes I have been using and wipe them carefully with a cloth as I retract them — to both clean and dry them. I repeat the procedure with a cloth on which I've sprayed silicone or a light-weight lubricant to prevent rusting.

First Steps

CARPENTRY BEGINS WITH a rule or tape measure and a pencil. I would no more think of setting off to work without a carpenter's pencil in my toolbox or carpenter's apron than I would think of leaving the house without my glasses and driver's license. This is one tool you should never have to buy. Every self-respecting lumberyard offers, as giveaways, pencils stamped with the name and logo of the yard or of a product sold there.

An ordinary pencil may be just a round column of

graphite embedded in a wood casing, but a carpenter's pencil is a cunningly designed eight-sided instrument with an oval column of lead. The casing is about ⅝ inch wide by ¼ inch thick and as long as a standard pencil; it stands up well to rough use at a construction site.

In cross section (seen easily at the end of the pencil), all eight sides of the perimeter are visible. Two parallel sides are much wider than the others, so the pencil won't roll off any piece of material you rest it on. (Your efficiency doesn't improve if you have to climb down from a ladder to retrieve a pencil that rolled off just as you reached for it.) I use this pencil mainly for marking rough framing. It fits snugly in the pencil pocket of my nail apron.

The thick lead of a carpenter's pencil is ideal for making clear marks on rough lumber, even wet lumber. The thickness also keeps the lead from breaking easily. I can't keep an ordinary pencil in my apron for twenty minutes of framing before bending in such a way that makes it snap, and I can't mark framing lumber as clearly as I want with an ordinary pencil without breaking the lead.

It takes a little practice to learn how to sharpen a carpenter's pencil. You don't want the point to be too sharp. I sharpen the broad sides of the lead, slightly trim the narrow ends so that the tip is about

⅛ inch wide, and mark with it parallel to its widest dimension. My sharpener is whatever utility or pocketknife is handy. I've seen others use chisels or block planes.

On exterior trim and siding or interior finish work, of course, I need a much finer marker. I once experimented with a mechanical pencil. I liked getting more lead with a simple twist of the case instead of sharpening a tip frequently by hand, but after a fair trial I concluded that, even for finish work, the lead was too fine and broke too easily.

A friend suggested I try his mechanical drafting pencil. It worked well, and the lead didn't break as easily as with the other mechanical pencil I tried. Sharpening it, however, required carrying a special sharpener that you rotate the pencil in. It was a nuisance — one more thing to keep track of in a trade that has many basic tools you need within reach.

Eventually I settled on using ordinary #2 wood pencils that I often sharpen with my utility knife. During a whole day of interior trim work, when I might need to sharpen my pencil from ten to fifteen times, a fresh blade in my utility knife is all I need. My jackknife is my backup sharpener.

One type I never use is a marker with a felt tip. I once saw a job where an installer had marked all of the drywall with a felt-tip pen. The marks bled through every kind of paint the contractor tried to cover them with.

I carry three wood pencils in my apron or toolbelt: a carpenter's pencil, a #2 pencil for finer marking, and a second, short #2 in a small compass. I never leave home without the compass, and I doubt that I ever do a day of carpentry without needing it for marking or scribing. An inexpensive compass, the kind children use in school, works well, even though it wears out and has to be replaced every few months. When my other pencils aren't handy, I use the pencil in my compass as a marker.

The bottom line is: always carry a pencil, not a crayon or chalk, and something that will sharpen it. If you want to guarantee a dark pencil line or mark, first wet the tip of the graphite. No pencil is too short. Toward the end of the day, when I'm reluctant to look for a new pencil, I use the one in my apron until it's nothing but a nubbin.

Cutting Remarks

I HAVE A close friend who remembers learning carpentry from his father, a professional carpenter. The father would supervise a measurement closely, then advise his son to "make the mark." If the mark, in the father's opinion, was too heavy, he would bark, "What are you trying to do — cut the board with the pencil?" My father wasn't nearly as stern, but he also wanted to get the right balance. Don't make a darker or deeper line or mark than you need, especially in finish work; every mark that is visible at the end of construction will have to be sanded off, painted over, or stained.

One of my sons and my father both helped me install clapboard siding on our new house a few years ago. My father would tell Bobby, "You better cut that because you marked it." He had learned from experience that no two carpenters mark the same, so there are apt to be problems if one person marks and another person cuts. Is the mark meant to be left, or split, or removed?

I prefer to use an arrow rather than just a line when marking freehand for a cut. A freehand line will never be perfectly straight, so there can be a question of what part of it to use as a guideline. The point of an arrow, however, is something that anyone can place pretty accurately. Usually I split the mark with the saw. If I want to give myself a margin of safety, I leave the mark; I can always shave off a little more if I need to. I never remove the mark entirely; if the measurement is accurate, taking out the mark will make the piece too short.

If you have to mark for another person to cut, you can devise a code. For example, a half-arrow with the arrowhead drawn only on the right side of the shaft can mean to leave the mark, while a half-arrow with the arrowhead on the left can mean to split the mark. Or whatever system works for you.

Since I'm right-handed, I always cut so that the waste piece is to my right. I mark the length with a light half-arrow (⌐). Thus my cut will ordinarily be just to the right of the point or will split it.

No matter what the task, even if it's rough framing, my philosophy is that a carpenter should measure and mark as accurately as possible. Take whatever time you need at this point; your diligence will pay off in every subsequent step of the job.

I read this bit of advice not long ago: "For good, accurate work, a pencil is used only for marks that indicate measurements that are not meant to be cut." The inference is that for marking cuts the craftsman should use an awl, a fine little tool that looks like an ice pick. Working at a bench, with every tool within reach, I might concur. Yet even at the bench I'm not quite that conservative. Used carefully, a pencil is an acceptable marker even in fine woodworking. A pencil mark is easier to find and return to than scratch marks from an awl. If my marking pencil is lost or broken I mark with an awl, if I have one with me, or with a pocketknife or utility knife, or even with a nail. But these marks won't be as easy to find again.

Marking awl

The other day, when I was running the edges of some boards through a jointer before ripping them to width at the table saw, the side opposite the side I was running was already smooth. If the unjointed edge is a really good one, you can run a board through the jointer and, unless you've marked the board, you'll go on to the next step and say, "Now which edge did I plane?" So I made a light little penciled X as a witness mark on the side I'd jointed. When I ran the board through the table saw, the pencil mark alerted me to put that side against the rip fence.

Pencil marks are valuable for more than just identifying where to cut; they are guides for a sequence of steps. I may look at a board and decide which face of it should show. Since I don't want to have to keep checking, I mark the side I've chosen. Even with finish lumber, I make a light mark that doesn't damage the board.

A-Huggin' and
A-Chalkin' Away

A CARPENTER CAN'T get very far without knowing how to lay out reliably straight lines. The longer the line contemplated, the more careful he has to be that it doesn't stray. Even in ancient Greece, a carpenter's toolbox or kit included lengths of cord or twine for snapping lines. At some point early in the evolution of carpentry, craftsmen began to store the twine on a stick or wood reel between uses.

In Greece, the marker of choice was ocher: iron oxide mixed with sand or clay to form a substance ranging from yellow to brown to red. Today we use powdered chalk derived from a soft limestone. The best-known display of the dazzling natural whiteness of chalk is at the celebrated seaside cliffs facing the English Channel at Dover. Against a relatively dark surface, natural chalk is an ideal marker, but against a light surface it can be hard to see.

When our ancestors wanted a dark marker, they resorted to the black carbon deposit on the end of a partially burnt stick of wood. We now accomplish the same purpose by using tinted chalk, which is marketed in either blue or red. I've used both, but I prefer red because it's easier to see. One disadvantage, however, is that red chalk sticks to whatever it touches — the surface you're marking, your hands, your clothes, everything. But even though it's messier, I still like its visibility.

When I first started working with my father, he always had pieces of solid chalk in the tray of his toolbox; each piece was a half-sphere a couple of inches in diameter. The technique was to set the line, then run a piece of chalk along it just before snapping. By the time I began carpentry for hire, the chalk box with a retractable line was in general use, so I don't recall ever seeing my father use the pieces of chalk he still carried.

He and I always used boxes with 100-foot lines. A chalk box works somewhat like a fishing reel. I pull the line out as far as the measurement requires (it is already chalked from the powder in the casing), place it, snap it, then rewind it, using the handle on the side of the box.

Most new chalk boxes come with lines of twisted cotton thread. We always removed the twisted line and replaced it with braided line. My father preferred to use a braided nylon line — fishing line, actually, a little heavier than cotton twine. It is a little harder to get nylon well chalked, but it holds more chalk than cotton twine and breaks less easily.

Chalk box with line

Where the line leaves the chalk box, there is a gasket (rubber, foam rubber, or felt) to prevent the loose chalk inside from spilling out. This feature needs to be checked regularly. If the gasket wears out from repeated contact with the line, or if it is dislodged and falls off or (even more likely) falls into the box, you can lose your supply of powder in a hurry. On some boxes, powder is poured into the box through the opening for the line; on others, there is a place to add powder on the opposite end. Chalk, like mustard, comes in plastic dispensers with slender tips to prevent spills when the box is refilled. Never fill your chalk box too full; the line will become difficult to pull out and rewind.

Ritual

My father taught me always to tap the chalk box just before I pulled the line out. It became a ritual with us. A slight tap of the box (with the exit hole pointing down) against the hammer hanging in my holster loosens the powder, allowing it to cascade toward the exit hole. This ensures that the line gets a thorough coating as I pull it out.

It's best to anchor the end of the chalk line where the marked line is to begin. The line has a hook on the end in case there is something to snag it on. It also has a tapered slot that can be slipped over a temporary nail. A carpenter working alone can anchor his line, run it out as far as about 16 feet, set it, pull it taut, and snap it himself. But when you need a snapped line of 20 or 30 feet or more, it's a two-man job.

In a two-man operation, the beginning of the line is still anchored. The first man pulls the line out to the end point and holds it tightly in place. He sights down the line to make sure nothing on the surface — nail heads, for example, or splinters — is interfering with the line. Especially when the line is to be snapped on a plywood surface, there are apt to be imperfections that can snag it. (When I was working with my father, tight meant *tight*. I wrapped the line a couple of times around my finger and then pulled on it until my finger hurt. If the line isn't really taut, the snap can go astray.)

The second man goes to the middle of the line and presses it straight down against the surface to be marked. The line has now been bisected into two shorter lines. The man in the middle snaps the lines, first on one side, then the other. If a third man is available, it is unnecessary to anchor the beginning point with a nail, but the procedure remains the same.

For the most foolproof snaps, take the line between the thumb and index or middle finger, draw it back perpendicular to the surface to be marked, and release it. If the line has been bisected, the midpoint is released by its holder. Before the line is removed, it is wise to examine the mark carefully to see if it is directly under the line. If it's not, rub out the chalk mark and snap again.

On many chalk boxes, you can lock the reel that holds the line. This feature allows a carpenter to pull the line tight by pulling on the box itself and to use the box to anchor its end of the line before snapping. I always pull on the line, not on the box, and I anchor the line with my fingers. If the line is not really tight on the reel and you pull hard on the box, you may tangle the line by drawing the outermost segment through some of the loose coils.

Gravity

So FAR I've been talking about lines snapped down against floors or up against ceilings. When I want to snap a line sideways onto a vertical surface, I have to consider the additional factor of gravity, which causes the line to sag slightly. Suppose I wanted to snap a 30-foot line across a wall. The technique I would use is much the same as the one for making a long floor mark. Having a second person bisect the line by holding it at the midpoint would be essential. The line should be pulled very tight indeed. Even so, unless I had an independent measurement to verify its true midpoint, I would ask the man in the middle not to press the line straight against the wall but to roll it up ever so slightly — by the thickness of the line or a little more — to compensate for the inevitable sag caused by gravity, even with a tight line. It's a judgment call, but I always assume a slight sag even if it's not visible.

One of the toughest challenges when using a chalk line is damp weather. Once the line gets wet, it doesn't leave very good marks. And every time a wet line is reeled back into the box it releases more moisture into the powdered chalk, which begins to deteriorate. Fortunately, I've never been in a situation when so much moisture got into my chalk box that the powder consolidated or clumped. But it could happen.

Sweeping any standing water off a surface to be marked will help preserve the quality of the chalking. At the end of a damp day, when I have been using my chalk line and know that the nylon is wet, I reel out the whole line at home and let it dry near a source of heat. By the next morning it is ready for use again. Don't leave a damp line coiled inside your chalk box unless you want to have poor chalking the next day.

Since I carry 100 feet of line in my chalk box but rarely snap a line longer than 40 to 50 feet, even with a helper, half the line on my reel might, theoretically, seldom get used. It is more typical than not, I think, that a carpenter will use the first several feet of his line over and over again until a length wears out and breaks off, whereupon he uses the next several feet; his line gradually gets shorter until it has to be replaced. I believe, however, that a chalk line is most effective when all of the line is used as regularly as possible. If I'm doing a series of snaps, I don't reel the line back into the box when the chalk fades; I pull out a fresh length, letting the used length or lengths dangle until I've used all of the line or finished the task.

Easy Does It

IF YOUR CHALK line is in good condition, you should be able to get at least five or six acceptable snapped lines before having to rechalk or to pull a fresh length out of the box. Don't snap the first line with full force or you'll waste much of the chalk. Lift the line only an inch or two from the surface and release it gently. Snap the line progressively harder as the coating of chalk thins. The farther the line is pulled up before snapping, the more important it is that it be lifted precisely perpendicular to the surface. The line will snap off course opposite the direction you strayed while lifting it.

If you snap the first mark with a fresh line harder than necessary, you may leave a puffy trail of chalk, which slightly obscures the center of the mark. When that happens to me, I find that blowing gently is better than brushing to remove the excess chalk without smudging.

You may occasionally want to snap a line that ends in a corner. If you try to anchor the line in the corner with your finger, you may not get as much tension as you want. I take a little block of wood about ¾ inch wide, ¼ inch thick, and 3 or 4 inches long, press it into the corner, and pull the line tight around it to solve the problem.

If I'm preparing to snap lines on an exterior wall as guides for installing siding, I first hammer in the nails that will anchor one end of each snap. I place the first nail squarely in the center of where the mark is to be. The remainder of the nails I place just slightly below where the center of the mark should go. I hook the metal clasp at the end of the line onto the first nail and snap the line. Instead of removing the clasp and placing it over the next nail, I leave it where it is and loop the line up over the next nail, and the next, always leaving the clasp on the first nail. On every snap after the first, the line looks high because it's looped over the nail rather than being centered on it. But I have already accounted for this difference when I set the nails lower, so I've saved a little time and made the operation smoother. This technique works whether I'm alone or with helpers.

Many times I've been up on scaffolding and wanted to know if a section of wall frame was straight. If I had a mason's line or ball of cord with me, it was in the tray of my toolbox, a ladder climb away. But my chalk line is always in my toolbelt. I frequently use it as a guideline rather than a marking tool. I fasten spacer blocks of the same width at the ends of the wall I'm appraising, stretch my chalk line tightly from one block to the other, and run a third block of equal width along the space between the line and the wall. This technique will reveal any places that are bowed in or out and need a brace to be brought into perfect alignment. I use my chalk line the same way when determining whether the floor of a deck is level. The little bit of chalk I might spread around isn't any bother at all.

The chalk line is a simple but versatile tool. Just remember to keep the box amply (but not overly) supplied with powdered chalk and to tap it lightly against your hammer before pulling out the line.

Misstep

THE ODDEST FALL I ever took happened many years ago on Nantucket in a garage I was converting into a workshop. I was framing the second-floor walls, working alone. It had been a damp day with occasional drizzle, so everything was wet. Carrying an armload of tools, I stepped onto a ladder sticking up through an opening in the deck so that I could climb down to the first floor. I don't remember exactly, but I suspect it was at the end of the day, which is when anyone is apt to be tired, hence a little less alert. Whatever the cause, I slipped on one of the top rungs and fell all the way down the ladder, feet first, toppling onto my left side as I hit the brick floor below. The end of one arm of the metal framing square I was carrying got between my body and the deck in such a way that it hit one of my ribs squarely on impact. Had it gone between my ribs, I could have been badly injured. As it was, the square bent into a *U*-shaped curve from the force of my crash landing.

I still have the square, and it's still bent, a token of a lucky fall. I've never been able to straighten it.

A Better Mousetrap

HOW A NEW tool gets established commercially is something of a mystery to me since I've spent my life as a carpenter, woodworker, and contractor, not a marketing manager. At any given moment, inventors are trying to devise new tools, or variations on familiar tools, in hopes of capturing a segment of the market. It's the Better Mousetrap Syndrome. Whether a new tool is a promising invention or a short-lived gimmick depends eventually on the judgment of consumers.

In the first issue of *This Old House* magazine, the editors featured a claw hammer. How, you ask, can anyone improve a claw hammer? This particular hammer was intended for homeowners more than professional carpenters, I think. The claw was designed to pull small nails as well as larger spikes. That's smart because homeowners are apt to use small nails. The hammer has a nice conventional wood handle, but its head is chrome steel as shiny as the bumper of an old Buick Roadmaster. If a customer likes glitter, the shininess alone might make the hammer a best-seller.

The striking face is triangular, to make it easier, says the manufacturer, to drive nails in corners and other tight places. Finally, there is a magnetic T-shaped recess in the cheek (the middle section of the hammer, between the claw and the striking face), where the head attaches to the handle; you can hold a nail in the recess and make an initial sideways strike with the hammer while your other hand holds the object receiving the nail.

I have one of these hammers in my workshop — a gift, to be sure — but I doubt that it will ever make its way into my toolbox and never into my toolbelt. While this hammer might seem a godsend to some, to me it's more of a gimmick. A nail set in my apron will let me nail into any tight corners with my round-faced claw hammer. I have pretty good eye-hand coordination, but I'm not sure I could swing a hammer sideways and start the nail where I want.

Still, for all I know the shiny hammer will be a bigger success than an innovative framer's square I tried and liked — and never saw again in a store. The conventional framing square is a simple but invaluable tool composed of two legs that meet at a right angle. In the old days it was always made of heavy steel, but now some are aluminum or stainless steel or another light metal. The longer leg is usually 24 inches on its outside edge and 2 inches wide, the shorter leg 16 inches on its outside edge and 1½ inches wide.

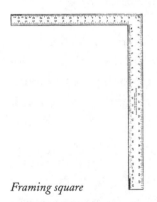

Framing square

On the innovative framing square I liked, the longer leg was the usual 24 by 2 inches, squared off at the open end. The other leg was shorter than usual, and its end was angled. The inside edge was the shorter, extending just 1 foot from where the two legs met. This configuration made rafter layout go faster. Roof pitch is expressed as inches of rise (the vertical distance) over each foot of run (the horizontal distance). It was easy to pivot off the 1-foot endpoint of the short leg to any prescribed pitch on the other leg — 2, 3, 4, 5 inches, etc.

There were calibrations for degrees as well as inches on the square, to facilitate marking angles expressed in degrees rather than the conventional inches/feet of pitch. There was also a slot in the long leg that was very useful for marking rafters that had to be, for example, shorter by half the thickness of the ridge beam. I could use the width of the short leg as though it were the thickness of a 2-by in measuring for rafters or studs.

I really liked this tool. Its only drawback was that it was made of aluminum, which is more flexible than steel and gives the tool some potential to get bent out of square. The slot in its long arm that made it more versatile only increased this potential. As it happened, the market did not appreciate this innovative square.

Once, the framing square was the only tool a carpenter used to lay out and mark cuts for rafters. (There was enough information on the square to figure out any type of rafter for just about any roof pitch if you had a pencil and basic math skills.) Now we have pocket engineering calculators or printed charts for calculating rafter lengths for various pitches, and we have the speed square. Carpenters use framing squares, at this juncture, mainly to mark sheets of plywood or wide boards, to lay out stair stringers, or to square up cabinets — in other words, in situations where the length of the legs gives this square a significant advantage over smaller combination squares.

But I still use a framing square for rafter and roof layout. I don't think it will ever be replaced in my work. Sometimes I use the chart on the square to calculate the length of the rafter or to lay out the angle for special cuts; at other times I break out my engineering calculator to do the math. It's unfortunate that some manufacturers no longer engrave the charts on their squares (and that very few carpenters these days can interpret the charts).

Handguns

JUST ABOUT EVERY carpenter I know carries a combination square, commonly called a c-square, in his toolbelt; he not only carries it but *uses* it — twenty, thirty, forty times a day or more. Most toolbelts have a special holder for the combination square. If yours doesn't, it's best to add one.

A combination square looks something like a pistol. The barrel of the pistol is a steel rule calibrated in inches and, on some models, in centimeters. The L. S. Starrett Company in Athol, Massachusetts — founded by Leroy Starrett, who invented the combination square in 1877 — makes them with rules an inch wide in lengths from 4 to 24 inches; the rules are calibrated in gradations of ⅛, ¹⁄₁₆, ¹⁄₃₂, and ¹⁄₆₄ inch. My own combination square, not a Starrett, is the 12-inch length most popular among carpenters. I suppose a 6-inch square would be my second choice. For most of the carpentry I do, the ¹⁄₁₆-inch calibration is the most useful.

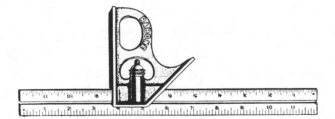

12-inch combination square

The grip or handle is perpendicular to the rule and fits over it far enough to overlap half its width; the top of the grip fits into a groove running down the middle of the rule. On most combination squares, the rule and grip can be completely separated, so that the rule can be used independently as a ruler or straightedge, but in others I've seen the groove isn't open at either end to allow the two parts to be separated. (One benefit of this latter kind is that neither part can get mislaid or lost by itself. The rule of a combination square still has some usefulness if the grip is lost, but the grip is totally useless without a grooved rule.)

It is the mobility of the grip along the groove in the rule that makes the combination square the flexible beauty it is. You can slide the grip to any desired setting, then lock it in place by turning a threaded knob attached to a spring mechanism. As you make a series of measurements and marks, it takes only a few seconds each time to adjust the setting.

One side of the grip forms a 90-degree angle with the rule. The other side forms a 45-degree angle, facilitating markings that are common in trim work. The difference in thickness between the slender rule (about ¹⁄₁₆ inch) and the thicker grip (between ½ and ¾ inch) makes it easy to hold the grip against one surface — the thickness, say — of a piece of lumber and measure and mark with the rule on the adjacent surface — the width or length.

Many combination squares have a 1- to 1½-inch removable metal pin stored in the base of the grip. It is a marking or scribing tool, a small scratch awl — handy for scratching a cutting mark. I use mine sometimes, but more often I use my carpenter's pencil or a utility knife because I want a more prominent mark than the metal pin can make.

Many squares also have a small spirit level built into the grip. I have to say that I don't depend on the level in my combination square if accuracy is paramount, for it gets some pretty rugged use. There's nothing worse for spirit levels than being dropped; they get concussions faster than NFL quarterbacks do on Sunday afternoons.

You can immediately grasp the value of combination squares for framing and trim work, carpentry functions that have taken up years of my life. In a few seconds a 2-by or a piece of finish trim can be marked for a cut that is, to use my shooting metaphor one last time, dead accurate. But don't ignore the many other applications of this tool. I suspect that if I tried to name all the possible uses of a combination square, the list would fill several pages of this book.

Let me identify just a few. It is an excellent scribing device. If you want to scribe a line down a board 3 inches from the edge, all you have to do is set the 90-degree side of the grip at 3 inches on the rule, hold the grip firmly against the board, and then, sliding the grip along, make a running mark with a pencil held against the end of the rule. It is equally easy to use the square to mark the reveal on a window frame. Using the 90-degree side of the grip again, you can check the end of a 2-by or other board for square after you've cross-cut it, or the edges of two boards to be joined when they need to be perfectly square. To check right-angle inside corners for accuracy, lock the 90-degree side of the grip at the very end of the rule and place the square against the corner. And, of course, the 45-degree side of the grip is ideal for marking any miter cuts that bisect the joint.

Losing a Prized Tool

IN A RECENT issue of *Fine Homebuilding*, a magazine I admire, Jefferson Kolle wrote about a Starrett combination square he inherited from his grandfather. The story caught my attention in part because I, too, have inherited some tools from my grandfather. Kolle's square was his favorite tool. One way he knew that it was excellent was that the calibrated marks along the blade were machined into the tempered steel, not merely etched on the surface. The blade was a hefty 3/32-inch-thick unchromed steel, which oxidized to a dark gray. When it got really dark from use or exposure when occasionally left out in the rain, Kolle rubbed the blade with a little oiled steel wool to brighten it up again. He mentioned that he uses his combination square to set the blade height on his table saw and to check blade angles — two more uses for my list. He also confesses to having opened paint cans with the end of the blade — a use that's *not* on my list — without damaging it.

One day Kolle finished a project and rather haphazardly piled his tools and extra materials into his truck. The next day, when he unloaded and sorted everything at his shop, his Starrett square was missing. Realizing that replacing it with a new Starrett would be costly, Kolle looked at a few less expensive makes. He tried to use a triangular square he had bought once on a whim, but nothing else seemed right. "Six months after completing the job where I lost my square, the customer called us back to finish the second-floor bath he hadn't had the funds for earlier. I was loading some material into his garage, and there on his newly installed pegboard was my combination square. I slipped the tool into my nail apron, right where it belonged, into the slot that I'd sewn in the leather."

I wish the story of every tool I've lost had such a happy ending. Kolle's square had the powerful combination of superior quality and sentimental value. Tools can indeed last for generations. If I were going to buy a top-of-the-line tool today, however, one I hoped my grandchild might someday treasure, I'm not sure I'd choose a combination square or other tool that I use regularly in the rough and tumble of framing. I don't use my combination square to open paint cans, but, like Kolle, I occasionally drop it from scaffolding, and it takes accidental abuse in the course of everyday carpentry. I'm satisfied to use a less expensive model knowing that, without complaint, I will have to replace it every several years.

Speed

WHEN I'M FRAMING a house, I make certain I have a speed square in my toolbox for measuring and marking the angles of rafters or any other pieces of the frame intersecting at angles other than 45 or 90 degrees. Usually made of cast metal but often of metal lighter than steel — aluminum, for example — a speed square is shaped like a right-angle triangle. It is small enough to be carried in my nail apron, so I don't need to look for my framing square when I'm doing a quick layout or checking the pitch or angle of a cut. (If I'm calculating a rafter length, I also need a printed chart relating pitch and rafter length, and in my experience this ingredient is often missing — either mangled by harsh exposure at the job site or left at home on my desk.)

The two short sides that form the 90-degree angle of the speed square are usually about 7 inches long. One of them has a flange edge about ¾ inch wide centered on the thickness of the body, which allows it to sit upright when set down on the flange. More to the point, the flange can be held against one surface of a board while the triangle is placed on the adjacent surface to check for squareness.

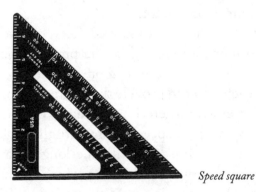

Speed square

I've already mentioned how the varying thicknesses of the grip and the blade of the combination square make the same operation easy. Given its shape, the speed square is obviously prepared to handle 45- and 90-degree measurements with ease. But in many cases the combination square can accommodate those angles as readily, and I usually have it in my toolbelt.

What makes the speed square essential is that it has degree calibrations, 0 through 90. Basically, on the speed square, the corner where the two short legs intersect becomes the pivot point. If I want to lay out a cut at 30 degrees, I hold the pivot exactly where I am going to make the mark, rotate the square until the calibration for 30 degrees is lined up with the long edge of the board, and mark the board along the short side of the square. The speed square is fairly accurate for the layout of whole degrees; anything finer may require a protractor.

The square is also calibrated for roof pitch. If I want to frame a roof with a 3-12 pitch — the rafter rises 3 inches every running foot — I need to cut the end of each rafter to provide the desired pitch. I hold the pivot exactly where I am going to cut the rafter and then rotate the speed square until the calibration for a 3 pitch is lined up with the long edge of the board; then I scribe the short leg, which doesn't have the flange because it is now in the proper position for a 3-12 cut. I can lay out the pitch with this square, but I need the instruction booklet or my engineering calculator to establish the length. This may sound daunting in print, but it is reassuring to know that every speed square comes with detailed instructions.

A Giant Tool

IT DOESN'T FIT in either toolbelt or toolbox. (Though I could strap it on my back like Robin Hood's longbow, I suppose.) But when I'm working on certain jobs, it's indispensable. It's a drywall square, the largest square I use, designed to help drywall installers quickly and accurately cut 4-by-8 and 4-by-12 sheets of drywall, but also useful for carpenters working with any sheet material up to 4 feet wide.

My drywall square is T-shaped. The long leg measures a full 48 inches below the crossbar of the T, is 2 inches wide, and is calibrated in fractions of inches on one side. The crossbar is 22 inches long. Sixteen inches of crossbar extend to the left of the long leg, and 6 inches extend to the right. The crossbar is ⅜ inch thick, the thickness of the thinnest sheet of drywall.

Often drywall is stored on its long edge. The drywall square gives me the option of resting the crossbar on the top edge of the sheet; the long leg extends the full width of the 4-by sheet but no farther. I can easily cut a sheet of drywall perfectly square by holding the short leg firmly on the top edge of the sheet and anchoring the bottom of the long leg with my left foot while running my mat knife along the edge of the square to score the drywall. I snap the sheet along the score line and cut from the back side along the crease. A square cut every time! I find this square equally valuable when I'm laying out 4-by sheets of plywood for decking or for kitchen cabinets or bathroom vanities.

Dealing with the Unknown

THE SQUARES I'VE discussed so far assume that a carpenter is dealing with a common angle such as 45 or 90 degrees or at least whole degrees. Occasionally I have to measure and mark an unusual angle — 11½ degrees, or 23 degrees 45 minutes, let's say — or even transfer an unknown angle from an old piece of wood to a replacement piece. For just such situations the sliding bevel square was invented. It consists of a handle and a blade that can be locked in any angle from 0 to 360 degrees. Some bevels have metal handles, but the one I carry regularly has a wood handle. Its blade is 6 inches long. I have another one in my shop, handcrafted by an acquaintance, with a rose-wood handle and a 12-inch blade.

Sliding bevel square

Bevel squares are sold by the length of the blade. A slot in one end of the handle permits the thin blade to pass right through it. I hold the handle against one side of the angle I want to reproduce, pivot the blade until it matches the other side, and tighten the thumbscrew to lock the handle and blade in position. Then I move the bevel square to the new piece and scribe on it the angle I've taken from the old piece. To help set the bevel square exactly where I want before I transfer the angle to mark it on another piece, I use an adjustable drafting square or a very accurate gauge I keep in my shop.

Plumb

ROGER HOPKINS, A stonemason who built the garden walls and terraces at my house, has traveled to Egypt a number of times to study the Great Pyramids. He differs with some authorities about how these amazing structures were built, but I think they all agree that the Egyptians used standing A-frames with weighted lines suspended from their apexes to judge whether the huge stones were vertically straight — or, as we say, plumb. (Imagine the consternation if, after months of labor, it appeared that the intended shape of a pyramid had gone askew.)

At first acquaintance, plumb seems a curious word. It doesn't have an association with everyday life the way references to horizontal, for example, make us think of horizons viewed in nature. A quick trip to a dictionary shows how a word can pick up meanings through its association with activities. The trail begins with the Latin *plumbum* for a heavy, pliable, but inelastic metal that we call lead. Its qualities made it the ideal material for weights. A lead weight attached to a line became a plummet, a mariner's device for sounding — determining the depth of water a boat is sailing in.

The pliability of lead made it suitable for pipes, so the tradesman who fashioned lead pipes into water delivery and waste removal systems came to be known as a plumber (literally, a leadman), a term that stuck long after plumbers abandoned lead for copper and synthetics. Eventually the word came to refer not just to the free-swinging weight used to test verticality but also to verticality itself.

Carpenters constantly refer to the qualities of level and plumb in a structure, but these concepts are hypothetical, not natural. Nature doesn't offer any perfectly flat horizons as a standard of level, and we have no direct way of knowing when we are looking straight up (vertically), in an extension of an imaginary line between us and the center of the earth, or straight down toward the center of the earth (perpendicularly). So we depend on instruments to tell us indirectly, based on the force of gravity. Gravity pulls the weight on a plumb bob toward the center of the earth; the line that holds it becomes a vertical measure.

Because of gravitational pull, a liquid resting in an immobile open container, not affected by air currents, will have a level surface; that is, a surface perpendicular to a line from the surface to the center of the earth. In the middle of the seventeenth century, someone figured out how to fill a clear oval vial almost full of liquid and seal it, leaving a little space for an air bubble. The bubble always rises to the highest possible point in the vial as the heavier liquid comes to rest. If the bubble is in the center of the oval, the vial is close to level. Its only immediate application was to telescopes. Two hundred years later, in the mid-1800s, bubble levels were first installed in bars of wood — or rails, as they are called — to assist carpenters and other tradesmen.

Our determinations of level or plumb are always approximate; the question is what degree of accuracy we aspire to. Air bubble levels are graded in arc-minutes; 60 arc-minutes equal a degree. Many levels are sold with a 45-arc-minute rating, meaning that the pitch of the level could be changed up to almost three quarters of a degree without causing any movement in the bubble. But you shouldn't be satisfied with a rating above 35 arc-minutes, and you can get vials accurate to 5 arc-minutes. The best carpentry today works to a finer standard of level and plumb, however relative, than our grandparents could imagine; the difference lies in the evolution of tools, not carpenters. It is a long jump from a handblown air bubble vial to a well-machined laser level. Still, we should not forget that our ancestors, using instruments no more sophisticated than those of the ancient Egyptians, built such marvels as the medieval castles and cathedrals of Europe and the Great Wall of China.

Premature Death

BUBBLE LEVELS ARE often called spirit levels because the liquid is a form of alcohol rather than water. Alcohol has a much lower freezing point than water, so it's possible to work with it in conditions so cold that water would freeze, expand, and break a glass or acrylic plastic vial. (I've worked in such conditions many times.)

Spirit level

The spirit level is one of the most delicate hand tools, but in framing and other rough carpentry it inevitably gets knocked about. A single mishap can damage it irreparably. Sometimes a blow that doesn't seem to have hurt the rail will affect the vial so that it is no longer accurate; checking your levels regularly is your only defense against using one unaware of its disability. One wintry day, I accidentally knocked my new metal 4-footer off a second-floor deck. It dropped a story and a half onto a concrete patio, where it broke into two pieces. Only two weeks old, it was gone forever! No matter how careful we are, we all drop our levels more than we like, but it's worth paying attention to how and where we put them down.

Caveat Emptor

CONCERN ABOUT THE accuracy of your levels should begin when you buy them. Even a brand-new level can be slightly (but fatally) off, as I have found in my own shopping forays. Here's how to check one — in the store, if possible; otherwise as soon as you get home. Place the level on a surface that looks nearly level and lightly mark the ends. The bubble will probably be a little off-center. Add pieces of paper or a thin piece of wood as a shim under the low end of the rail until the bubble reads perfectly level. (Do your best to look straight down on the vial as you read it; if there is any significant angle to your line of vision, you will misread the location of the bubble in relation to the guide marks on the vial.)

Next, turn the rail end for end, being sure to set it down at the same marks with the shim in its original position. If you don't get the same reading with the rail reversed, reject that level and try another one. I think you'll be surprised at how many levels fail this simple test. (I heartily recommend going to the trouble of returning a level that doesn't check out.)

Plumb can be checked the same way on a convenient vertical surface, except that the shim has to be held in place carefully to guarantee that it's constant when you reverse the rail. This test is equally appropriate any time you have reason to doubt the accuracy of your level. I check my spirit levels regularly to guard against the possibility that I've knocked them out of balance without being aware of it.

Trust Me

No spirit level is 100 percent dead-on accurate over long distances. The longer the distance, the larger the margin of error. If I take my longest level, a 4-footer, and make a straight 48-foot line by marking twelve continuous segments, each checked carefully to make sure it is level before I mark it, and then I check a hypothetical line from one end to the other with a more refined instrument, such as a builder's level or a transit, I will probably find a difference of

½ to 1½ inches from the high end to the low. And that's with a good level!

I've taken my 4-footer and gone carefully around the perimeter of a kitchen, checking the floor for level. It seemed fine. But a transit measurement of the same floor would find it ⅛ inch off. The error lies partly in the tool, partly in the user. I've seen experienced carpenters carrying levels they've used so long that the edges were rounded off. The wear and tear had to affect accuracy, but many carpenters hate to part with old, familiar tools. In fact, they often compensate for their shortcomings. A savvy carpenter who has knocked his level out of alignment may figure out precisely where the bubble should sit off-center when the rail is in fact level. It takes years of using tools daily to gain the confidence implied in such a strategy; an average person working around the house might better take the loss and replace a level that is out of kilter.

Measure for Measure

SINCE 1850, TOOL inventors have more than made up for the slow pace of their predecessors in adapting the spirit bubble from telescopes to portable carpenters' tools. There is now an astonishing array of tools — of every size, type, and material — to measure level and plumb for carpenters, plumbers, masons, and mechanics. If I kept a fair sample of what's available in my toolbox, there would be little room for anything else.

My favorite levels have solid cast metal rails. I'm not sure what the metal is; it's far lighter than iron, but it's not aluminum. For durability and ease of handling, I prefer solid construction to the extruded I-beam rails usually made of aluminum. As second choice, I would turn to what is generically called a mason's level — a wood rail edged in metal to prevent the edges from wearing enough to throw the leveling function off. Often the wood is mahogany and the metal, brass. I've used this type of level quite a lot and have one now that is very accurate.

The vials in spirit levels can be either acrylic resin or glass, plain or protected by an additional layer of transparent material. If you browse in your favorite hardware store or home center, you will see that some of the vials have straight oval sides and others, arched sides. I like arched vials better. You can tell something about the age of a level by looking at the vials. Older levels often have separate vials for reading off each long edge of the rail; newer levels have single vials that read accurately in a 360-degree rotation.

Some levels have vials that are adjustable, and

replaceable if broken. Others have vials glued in place. I prefer the permanently fixed vials because the adjustable ones get knocked out of alignment more easily. Once they're out of adjustment, it can take a lot of tinkering to make them right again. My preference means that if I accidentally break a vial, or even knock it badly out of balance, I have to replace the whole level: all the more reason to take good care of my tools.

Strictly on the Level

I USUALLY CARRY three levels, an 18-inch, a 28-inch, and a 4-footer. Since nothing except length of rail distinguishes one from another, you can easily deduce that I use them in different situations. I use the 4-footer for plumbing walls and when I need a straightedge that is from 1 to 4 feet long (for markings up to a foot, I use the rule of my combination square as a straightedge). The 28-inch model is particularly useful for leveling doorjambs (an average door is 30 inches wide) and for setting smaller cabinets. The 18-inch level stays in my toolbox until I run into a tight corner, where its shorter length is a virtue.

Spirit levels are more useful to me in checking

plumb than level. When I put a wall up, I sometimes use a level to plumb it. I could use a plumb bob, of course, but when I'm doing a quick, small job I reach for my level. It takes only a second to grab it and hold it against a stud, which is less trouble than getting a plumb bob out of my toolbox, unwinding the string, using it, rewinding the string, and finally putting it away.

If I stand on a stepladder and hold the string at the top of a wall, I have to wait for the plumb bob to stop swinging, then spot the point of the bob from 6 feet away or more; a reading under such conditions is less reliable than the one I get with a level. To get a reliable plumb bob reading, I would have to hang the string from the top of the wall (usually from a nail) so that I could view the point of the bob from close to floor level.

In general, I try to complete a task well, but also as quickly as possible and with the fewest tools consistent with efficiency. Every tool used is one more thing to get out, keep track of, take care of, and put away. As I look at it, this principle, vital to the full-time carpenter, applies equally to the homeowner who uses his tools only occasionally.

The Straight
and Narrow

AN ACQUAINTANCE WHO has recently done research on levels told me that many spirit levels are
now manufactured with a very slight arc in the rail —
to prevent readings from being thrown off because
sawdust particles on or imperfections in the surface
have lifted the level above the true plane of the surface. I haven't bought a new level for a year or two,
but I hope that any arc in a level I buy is so small as
not to affect a reading based on less than the entire
rail. If an arc were substantial, the level would be reliable only for readings from end to end. All carpenters frequently use a level to check surfaces shorter
than the rail; the unused part of the rail juts out into
space.

The surface I want to check is more frequently
longer, not shorter, than my rail. If I'm framing an
8-foot wall, my longest level, the 4-footer, can read
plumb for only half the height of the studs. I can take
a reading on the bottom half, then slide the level up
to the top half, but breaking the span into segments

already begins to court error. Since most 2-bys used as studs aren't perfectly straight, it would be best to get a single reading from top to bottom. What I need is an 8-foot straightedge that I can set my level against and know that I'm getting a reliable reading for the whole stud. (Another job might require a shorter or longer straightedge, but 8 feet is apt to be the most useful length.)

So, as many framers do, I cut one from an 8-foot sheet of ¾-inch plywood. Four inches is a good width for a straightedge. Be sure to cut it from the edge of the sheet because the factory's edge is reliably straight; always place your level against that edge.

The two long sides of the straightedge must be perfectly parallel. If you cut the 4-inch-wide strip on a table saw, you should be able to get a nice parallel cut. Even a circular saw with a guide fence might suffice if you saw carefully. If your only option is to saw freehand, the edge you cut may be a little wavy.

In that case, you should take the extra step of cutting two blocks of wood, each ¾ by ¾ by 4 inches. Glue and nail a long side of each block to an end of the long side of the straightedge that you cut yourself. The blocks can be planed or sanded, as necessary, until they are exactly parallel with the factory-cut edge. Now you have a straightedge that is true at each end of the side you cut yourself and reliable on the entire length of the factory-cut side. An imaginary line drawn from the outer edge of one block down to the outer edge of the other will be parallel to the factory-cut edge. Place the edge with blocks against any surface you want to check for plumb, confident that a level placed against the factory-cut side will give you an accurate reading.

Suppose, however, you're building a deck with 12-foot joists and you want to make sure they are level before you install the flooring over them. Always sight along the edge of any piece of wood you're working with to check for straightness. It would be unusual if you found that all the 2-bys you bought for joists were perfectly straight. Probably they were straight when first sawn, but as they dry further they warp a little.

An 8-foot plywood straightedge isn't going to do the job. What you can do is sight some 12-foot boards until you find the odd straight one and make it your straightedge. The joists are always installed with any convex edges facing up — referred to as putting the crown up. You can't, therefore, determine whether a joist is level as a whole by putting a 12-foot straightedge directly against it; any crown will throw the reading off. Instead, you can put the same kind of blocks on your 12-foot straightedge that I recommended for your 8-foot straightedge if it was cut with a handsaw.

Your goal is to be sure that the ends of every joist

are level with each other, no matter how much crown there is in between. Place the blocks of the altered straightedge against the ends of a joist and lay your level on the unblocked side. For exterior decking, you may want one end of each joist to be slightly lower than the other, to allow rainwater to run off. If the deck is attached to the house, you should pitch the deck slightly away from it. By making one block of your makeshift straightedge slightly thicker than the other, you can give the deck joists a uniform pitch.

The block feet on a straightedge are one of a carpenter's best tricks; they neutralize the irregularities in whatever you're trying to level or plumb. My father always used to carry a 6-foot level. Because of its length, I believe, it was the easiest to knock out of accuracy. For that reason I use long straightedges combined with shorter levels.

Scope

WHEN I NEED to check a foundation, I use a builder's level, a simpler version of the transit that surveyors use. It consists of a telescope, like a rifle scope, attached to a base that can be mounted on a tripod. The tripod must be set firmly so that its legs won't shift while the scope is being used. The legs can be adjusted to make the base level or close to level. Three or four leveling screws in the base allow further adjustments until the one or two spirit bubbles in the base read level.

To guarantee overall accuracy, I recommend adjusting the base until it is level, then swiveling it 180 degrees and checking the vials again. Once the base is level, all readings through the scope will reflect the same level as long as the tripod doesn't move. The scope swivels in an arc of 360 degrees as it defines a level plane extending from the scope in all directions. A person moving about the site with a reference marker — a freestanding calibrated rod, a carpenter's rule or tape measure, or a length of wood — takes measurements based on sightings from the swiveling scope.

Boutique Tools

I've used electronic levels, but they haven't yet replaced any of the spirit levels in my toolbox. The electronic mechanism is housed in a module with a read-out panel; the unit, about 6 inches long, is purchased separately and can be inserted in any of several different lengths of rails sold by the same manufacturer. One size fits all. If the mechanism goes out of adjustment, you can (as described in the manual) recalibrate it electronically.

The first electronic levels beeped when a measured surface was level or plumb. I think this method was disconcerting to carpenters, who are used to visual images. I confess that I didn't like it myself; it's hard to learn to trust your ear when you're accustomed to using your eyes.

But trust the marketing instincts of tool manufacturers. A second generation of electronic levels has simulated bubbles on the read-out panels so that you can make a visual determination. And I've heard, but haven't seen for myself, that one level has both an electronic module and an old-fashioned spirit vial implanted in the rail. Have your cake and eat it, too!

The most impressive feature of an electronic level is that you can set it for pitches other than level or plumb. For instance, if you're laying drainpipe and you'd like to have ¼-inch pitch to the foot to cause gravitational flow, you can program the module so that it reads level when you have reached that specific pitch. You can accomplish the same purpose less elegantly with a conventional spirit level by taping a shim to one end of its rail; when the pipe you're measuring lies at the pitch you want, the shimmed rail will read level. A ½-inch-thick block taped to the end of a 4-foot level, to give one example, will make the bubble read level when the pipe has a pitch of ⅛ inch to the running foot.

Roof pitches can likewise be programmed into an electronic level. When I framed a variation of an eyebrow window on my new house, I found an electronic level very useful. I knew the pitch I wanted — I believe it was a 5-inch rise every 12 inches — so I strung a line and then adjusted it with the level on it until I got the desired reading. I could have used a framing square calibrated for roof and rafter pitches, but the electronic instrument made the job go swiftly.

A cross section of an electronic level's rail is triangular rather than the familiar rectangle of spirit levels. One limitation of electronic levels is that readings can be taken off only one side of the rail. I find this aspect very inconvenient compared to the ability to read a spirit level off either edge or side.

I've heard that rectangular electronic levels are on the way. Maybe a conventional shape will appeal to more carpenters. But maybe they will be put off by the difference in price. You can buy an excellent spirit level for about a quarter of the cost of an electronic one. Some manufacturers offer cases for electronic levels like the covers for tennis racquets — pretty ritzy for a carpenter.

Laser levels are expensive, too, and therefore not

certain to become prominent on the job or in the shop. Lasers establish level planes with beams of visible or invisible light; toolmakers have adapted laser technology to the scale of carpentry. Now there are combination laser-spirit levels on the market. After you center the bubble, you press a button to activate the laser beam. It will project a small dot of colored light up to a few hundred feet away on a plane with the measuring surface of the rail.

The reliability of the laser projection depends, of course, on the rail placement; any deviation from true level will be increased in proportion to the length of the laser projection. For that reason, these combination levels are made with bubble vials accurate to 5 arc-minutes. I prefer to use a builder's level over the longer distances the combination level is designed for. I would like to have a bubble vial accurate to 5 arc-minutes, but probably not intensely enough to buy the expensive laser capacity I would rarely use.

Another laser invention is an instrument that establishes a continuous line of light — a level plane — around an arc of 360 degrees. It's as if the scope of a builder's level projected a light as it swiveled in a circle and the line of light remained visible. You can set this instrument on a tripod, adjust it to level, and project a line of light around a room where you want to install wainscoting or moldings. I can think of several other applications, but when I consider whether I do any of them frequently enough to justify having another expensive tool, I know the answer.

Afloat

SINCE WATER SEEKS its own level, you can fill a long tube with water and run it between two points where you want to establish level marks; if there are no air bubbles to affect the movement of the water, it will settle at the same level in both ends. The ends need to be transparent; a little coloring in the water helps, too. I find that it's hard to check the absolute location of any point with a water level, but it can be useful if I'm trying to establish approximate level over a distance beyond the capacity of my other levels and if I don't have easy recourse to a more refined instrument, such as a builder's level.

I consider water levels, laser levels, and builder's levels as tools, not to locate an exact point, but to establish coordinated points from which I can measure up or down to get specific points to mark for construction. That's how I've used these tools — to make reference points. They are all much more useful as leveling devices than in establishing plumb. When you come right down to it, the spirit level in a rectangular rail is the most versatile for going back and forth from level to plumb.

Midgets

THERE IS A short spirit level, several inches long, called a torpedo level. A plumber might use it to check the pitch on pipes he is installing when he doesn't need to be perfectly accurate, just heading in the right direction. Levels that have been developed with plumbers' needs in mind have a groove running down one side so that plumbers can set them on a horizontal length of pipe and not have to hold them in place constantly.

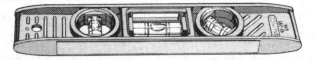

Torpedo level

The removable module in electronic levels can be used independently as a torpedo level. I've almost never used one because I usually work on long enough surfaces that my 18-inch level is the shortest I need. As I've explained, the shorter the level and the longer the surface being measured, the greater the margin of error. So I'm more apt to use a medium or long level held against an even longer straight-edge. Around the house, a torpedo level could be useful for hanging pictures, but that's about as complicated a job as I want it to do.

The string level consists of a small bubble vial held in a metal or plastic case that is threaded onto a string. Masons often use it in setting a line for laying a course of brick or block. I've seen carpenters use it, but even in rough framing I don't trust it to provide the degree of accuracy I want. The straightness of the string depends on the tension placed on it, which makes this tool too variable for my taste. But I can see how it might be very useful to landscapers.

I've seen but never owned a short level with Velcro straps attached. A person working alone who needs to maneuver a vertical post into plumb can strap the level to the post and adjust it with both hands until the level reads plumb; on occasion, I would find such a tool extremely convenient.

Finally, there is a small circular level called a bull's-eye; it fits easily into the palm of your hand and reads in all directions at once. When you get the bubble completely inside the circle marked in the center of the round vial, you have achieved more than level on a single axis defined by a straight line; you have achieved level in a 360-degree plane.

(To test your own steadiness easily but effectively, pick up a spirit level in a rail and try to hold it exactly level in front of you for several seconds. So far, so good. Now pick up a bull's-eye level in your palm and try to manipulate the bubble into the circle and keep it steady for several seconds. This test is much more difficult; the little bubble can be quite perverse. If you pass, your manual steadiness is excellent.)

Theoretically, the plane of a bull's-eye extends infinitely in all directions, but in practice, the farther you get from the instrument, the less reliable the reading. Since a bull's-eye is only an inch or two in diameter, it isn't much help in checking an average floor for level. But if I ever make a billiards table, this level could be invaluable. What could be worse than seeing billiard balls move freely because the table has a slight but fatal pitch.

None Simpler

WHAT A GREAT tool a plumb bob is! It's nothing more than a length of string attached to a pendant that tapers to a point; when the pendant hangs free, its point is an extension of the string. There are no mechanical parts to wear out — only a string to replace occasionally. The pendant has to be heavy enough to pull the string taut and to keep it from being affected by mild air currents. Older models are shaped like knobs, but many of the mass-produced ones available today are cylindrical, tapering to a point at the end.

You can find plumb bobs in the toolboxes of several trades. Surveyors use them constantly. A friend once gave me a compact little brass plumb bob with a reel for the string comparable to the reel in a chalk box. It was made specifically for elevator installers, who have to check long shafts for plumb; the reel saved them the time and effort of wrapping the string by hand each time around the bob or a stick.

Since the case of many chalk boxes is shaped like a diamond, with a pointed end opposite the hole for the string, some carpenters use their chalk boxes as plumb bobs: the box becomes the bob. Not I. I don't trust the box to hang straight down from the string, and I don't think the box comes to a fine enough point for reliable measuring and marking.

Bob to hang on a reel

What my father and I have often done, however, is to wind the plumb string on an old chalk box reel. Carpenters are always looking for ways to improve a technique. If you use a plumb bob only once or twice a day, it's still worth adopting a better way to rewind the string. A reel does the job quickly and relatively uniformly, and you don't have to think much about the process. If you don't rewind by hand carefully enough, the line gets snarled. Our ideal home for the plumb string was an old chalk box missing its gasket, which keeps the extra chalk from falling out, but with a working reel.

A typical bob is 3 to 5 inches long. Some have replaceable tips. A sharp tip is desirable because it leaves a reference mark on most surfaces it touches. I've seen illustrations for plumb bobs with 1/16-inch-diameter holes in the tip. Batteries and bulbs inside the bob send a light through the tip. This feature would be useful if you often worked in dimly lighted spaces, but I don't think its value would compensate for the loss of a sharp point to show where to make a precise mark.

Just as my father and I preferred nylon fishing line to the natural fiber cord of most chalk boxes, so I have come to prefer a different kind of string for plumb bobs. The manufacturer often supplies plumb bobs with strings made of twisted thread; when you let them out, they spin until the string is fully unwound, getting slightly longer in the process.

When you're transferring a marked point from a ceiling to its mirror point on the floor below, you want the point of the bob to be very close to the floor. If you put the point near the floor before the bob has stopped spinning, it is apt to drop just far enough before it is still to require shortening the line a fraction of an inch. When I buy a new plumb bob, I immediately replace the twisted string with braided thread, which steadies very quickly.

A year or two ago, a manufacturer sent me a plumb bob with several attractive features. The string is stored on a reel inside a plastic case that resembles the case of a metal rule. A plunger on the case allows you to push a pin into any reasonably soft surface such as wood, drywall, or plywood, attaching the case where you want to drop the bob. If you want to test a metal column or structure for plumb, there is a magnet on the case to hold it steady at the right place. A friction device on the reel prevents the bob from falling farther than you've pulled the string out, and there's an automatic rewind button. This plumb bob is most useful when I'm working alone (frequently) and need a measurement that ordinarily requires two people — one to hold the string at the top, the other to mark the point below.

When I first started using a plumb bob regularly, I was framing houses. After the exterior walls, roofs, and interior walls were framed out, the joists installed and ceilings strapped, the crew turned to the interior partitions. First, we marked all of them on the floor with chalk lines. Some carpenters then build the partition frames on the floor, raise them so that they stand where they should on the snapped floor lines, and use a level to adjust the standing wall for plumb before nailing the top plate to the ceiling and to any intersecting walls. This method, however, will not necessarily yield a wall frame that is either perfectly plumb or straight.

The better way is to snap lines on the ceiling strapping that mirror the chalk lines on the deck — ideally a two-man operation. One holds the plumb string up to the strapping where the plate will eventually be nailed. The second, at deck level, gives the first one directions until the bob is hanging just where it should above the floor line, whereupon the first man marks the ceiling. Enough marks are made so that intersecting lines can be snapped on the ceiling to mirror all the lines on the floor. Then the partition frame is made, raised, and adjusted along its length until it conforms everywhere to the snapped lines. The wall is reliably plumb and straight. The alternate method depends on the reliability of your spirit level — which is less reliable than the plumb bob — and on the straightness of the studs used as guides for the level; if the studs are slightly bowed or twisted, they will throw the wall off.

When I'm putting up a wall by myself, I drive in a nail partway where I want to hang a plumb bob. Then I hook the plumb string up over the nail and back down to where I am kneeling by the bob. For a few measurements, this fairly laborious technique works well. Since a typical wall is 8 feet high or more, I make sure I have at least 20 feet of string, because the line has to go from the bob near the floor up over the nail at ceiling height and back down to where I'm kneeling.

A few years ago, I used a plumb bob to mark the corners of the foundation that an excavator was about to dig for our new house. A surveyor had earlier staked out the house to the architect's specifications. Since the process of excavation would destroy any stakes placed precisely at the corners, the surveyor placed them 20 feet off the corners. But I had to put temporary stakes at the actual foundation corners to guide the excavator. I hooked my 50-foot tape to a nail on the offset stake, pulled it out 20 feet, hung my plumb bob from the 20-foot mark on the tape, and let the point of the bob, after it steadied, touch the ground, where its sharp tip made enough of an impression to show me where to pound in a temporary stake.

Hanging the doors to the house, some months later, was also a project I did myself. A carpenter can hang a plumb bob down the center of a doorway and measure off the line to the sides of the doorjamb wherever he wishes. So long as the measurements are the same on each side of each point on the line, he knows the door frame is plumb. I found my special plumb bob with the reel, plunger, and pin very useful. The housing for the string is designed so that the string is $2\frac{3}{8}$ inches from the surface that the pin is pushed into. I fastened the case to the top of each jamb and adjusted the jamb as necessary so that it stood $2\frac{3}{8}$ inches from the string wherever I measured.

This simplest of tools is so useful that I have practically stopped using levels for interior framing. A length of braided cord, a sharp bob a few inches long, and a chalk line are all I need to make a house straight and plumb.

The Better the Tool, the Better Beware

THE BEST CROSSCUT saw I ever carried in my toolbox had a stainless steel blade. Most saws are made of regular steel, of varying quality. My stainless blade had two advantages. It resisted rust from exposure in all seasons and weather conditions better than a regular steel saw blade, and, because the stainless steel was harder than regular steel, it held its sharpness or edge better and longer; it didn't need to be sent off for sharpening very often. Because of its quality, ironically, I had to be careful to send it to a sharpener who knew how to work with stainless steel.

In the end, I was not the only carpenter who thought my saw was the best I'd seen. I bought the saw when I was foreman of a framing crew; one day it was missing from my toolbox. I knew I hadn't mislaid it — a common way to lose good tools. Someone had deliberately taken it from my box. Perhaps that's one of the reasons I eventually started my own business, where I could work either by myself or with a few other tradesmen I knew and trusted.

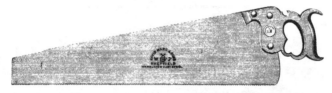

Crosscut saw

Since I carry regular steel saws now, I try to wipe the blades down at the end of the day either with a dry rag or, even better, a rag dampened with a little machine oil or another rust-inhibiting lubricant. On a hot day, just the sweat from your hands on the saw can contribute to the rusting of the blade if you don't rub it down before putting the saw away.

From Father to Son, from Four Saws to Two

My dad always carried four basic handsaws in his toolbox: two ripsaws and two crosscut saws. I carry only two crosscut saws. These days I rarely see anyone carrying a ripsaw at construction sites. But I do know some cabinetmakers and cabinet installers who still like ripsaws for specific tasks — for example, to trim stiles (the upright outer structural members of a door, window, cabinet, or other structure) where cabinets meet a wall that is not perfectly plumb. They believe they can make the cuts as quickly, cleanly, and accurately with a fine ripsaw as with a jigsaw or even a plane.

A ripsaw is meant to cut wood parallel to its grain, or "with" the grain. On most boards, the grain runs with the length. The ripping cut is longer (often considerably longer) than a cut across the width of the piece. Therefore the ripsaw quickly became an endangered species when the power circular saw joined the carpenter's arsenal. Who wants to rip a 2-by-10 by hand when the circular saw does it as cleanly and effectively, works much faster, and requires far less expenditure of energy?

Wood offers less resistance when cut with the grain than against it. Ripsaw blades consequently have larger and fewer teeth per running inch than crosscut saws. The teeth, which are slightly thicker than the rest of the blade, literally chip away the wood with edges that are filed straight across like the cutting edge of a chisel. Unless the kerf (channel) the saw is cutting is slightly wider than the blade itself, the saw would quickly bind from the friction generated from the wood pressing on each side. Even so, binding can be a problem on a long cut with a ripsaw. Sometimes it helps to insert a nail or a thin shim of wood into the kerf a foot or two behind where the saw blade is cutting just to hold the kerf open enough to prevent binding.

Crosswise

THE CIRCULAR SAW has had a considerable effect on my use of a crosscut saw, for I now principally use the power saw to cut studs, rafters, and other framing members to length. These cuts across the grain were once made routinely (if a little more slowly) with crosscut saws. A crosscut blade slices through the fibers of wood as a knife cuts through the fibers of a piece of meat. The teeth do not extend straight out from the saw blade like ripsaw teeth; they alternately angle out to one side of the blade or the other. The saw thus cuts a kerf that is slightly wider than the saw blade.

To see this construction, hold up a saw blade so that its back or spine is closer to your eye and sight across the blade; you will see the tips of the teeth sticking out in alternating directions. The teeth of a crosscut saw are smaller and set closer together than those of a ripsaw; they are beveled on both sides like the blade of a knife rather than filed into the chisel-like edges of ripsaw teeth.

I carry an eight-point and a ten- or twelve-point crosscut saw in my toolbox. Each has a 26-inch-long blade attached to a wood handle by screws. The saws are virtually identical except for the number of teeth per running inch (points) on the cutting side of the blade: the more points, the finer the cut. So I use the eight-point saw for rough framing and reserve my ten-point saw for finish carpentry — making and installing cabinets, for example. But if I crosscut most lumber with a circular saw, when do I actually use a crosscut handsaw? Not frequently, but when I do I'm very glad it's available.

Rafters and joists sometimes need to be notched. A lot of carpenters run the circular saw in both directions of the notch so that the wood being removed falls out. But if you do that, the curved blade of the circular saw is cutting past the mark, slightly weakening the board and resulting in a not very elegant bit of craftsmanship. I was taught to use the circular saw only until the outermost point on the curve of the blade reaches the mark of the notch, then to complete and even out the cut with a crosscut saw. An eight-point saw is ideal for such a task. It cuts quickly even through framing material that isn't completely dry (a frequent condition).

When I'm cutting a notch in a windowsill, in a piece of finish trim to fit around a post or into a corner, or in flooring material, out comes my ten-point crosscut saw. I would ordinarily use a jigsaw for such a cut, but sometimes it isn't worth getting out a power saw just to make a couple of cuts.

Of Chefs
and Carpenters

IF YOU WATCH an accomplished carpenter, you'll
see that he uses saws the way a chef uses knives.
When a chef is chopping vegetables, he is careful not
to put his fingertips at risk. He tucks them in a little
so that the knife comes down parallel to the length of
the finger from the tip to the first joint. An off-target
stroke should then glance harmlessly off his finger-
nails.

A carpenter should be as careful of his hands as a
chef. Starting a crosscut, I grip the piece with my fingers far enough away from the mark that I can barely
touch the blade with the outward flexed knuckle of
my thumb. My knuckle will be a guide for the blade
until I get the cut well started. The grip I have suggested puts my knuckle against the side of the blade
a little above the teeth. Likewise, when I want to rip
a piece of wood along the grain, I grip the end of the
board with my fingers and let the tip of my thumb
rest lightly on the blade of the ripsaw in back of the

teeth. In both cases, I position the blade just a hair to the waste side of the mark.

The Unkindest Cut of All

GETTING A CUT started properly is the most difficult part of the job. The saws my father taught me how to use, and that his forebears passed on to him, mainly do their cutting on the push motion rather than the pull. But it's easier to get the cut started with pull or back strokes than with push strokes. A pull stroke using the wider end of the blade near the handle gives you the most control; a few successive pull strokes may be necessary to establish enough of a kerf that push strokes will work without the blade's buckling.

There is no substitute for practice in the craft of sawing. The more control of the handsaw a carpenter has, the farther toward the narrow end of the blade he can work without worrying that it will buckle. An expert will get the cut established with a single pull followed by long, smooth strokes that cut through the wood swiftly and gracefully. A novice may give the impression that he is trying to accomplish the cut mainly through physical force. But an experienced carpenter lets the saw do the work.

Long, smooth strokes of moderate force, in which the blade stays in contact with the wood through the whole push motion, will accomplish more than shorter strokes applied with greater force. You should avoid buckling the blade at practically all costs. A severe buckle can throw a saw out of line and make it difficult to get a straight cut no matter how carefully it is used.

All's Fair That's Square

AN APPRENTICE CARPENTER, I've observed, usually learns to saw straight — that is, he can keep his saw accurately on the line marked for cutting — before he learns to saw square so that the ends and sides of the board consist only of right angles. But in most applications it is just as important that the thickness of the board be square to the width as that the length or width have straight edges. It's quite possible to make a cut that is straight only to find that the kerf has angled away from squareness — a problem difficult to remedy without ruining the dimensions the board is supposed to have.

It helps to use the right technique. The carpenter's body should be poised over the board so that the natural motion of his arm, from shoulder through elbow to wrist and handgrip, is going to drive through the cut at a right angle to the face of the wood. Simple practice and observation of the results tell the carpenter whether he has positioned his body a bit too much to one side of the cutting line or the other to get a square cut. With practice, eye-hand coordination develops, and the ability to make a square cut becomes habitual.

There is, however, a second requirement for square cutting: the tool itself. A handsaw can perform only as well as its condition permits. If, for instance, you happen to hit a hidden nail that blunts the teeth of a crosscut saw bending in one direction from the blade, you will find that the saw automatically favors the sharper set of teeth bending the other direction; the saw itself will then tend to cut off-square. You can check the configuration of the teeth by holding the blade so that you can sight along them, and you can test their sharpness by holding the saw so that its teeth face a direct light. If you see light reflecting off the tips of the teeth you will know they are blunt and dull. You can use this technique to check any tool with a sharpened edge.

A poorly sharpened saw can be as frustrating as a dull one. My dad could sharpen and adjust his saws. But I send mine through a lumberyard to a shop where they are put on machines that uniformly balance and sharpen the teeth. Lumberyards often provide this service for their customers.

It pays to buy good saws. The best ones have blades of tempered steel or other alloys that are tough enough to hold an edge and yet flexible enough to reduce the tendency to buckle. A good blade is tapered very slightly from the teeth to the spine; making the blade's body narrower than its teeth lessens the chance it will bind between the two faces of a kerf. So buy the best saws you can afford, send them out for machine sharpening as necessary, and practice until you feel that you have mastered each one.

Imports

YOU CAN GET very fine European handsaws, but for both rough and finish carpentry I can get all the performance I need from comparable American saws. However, Japanese saws have crept into my life — not quite into my toolbox but into my workshop for woodworking. Their blades are very thin, which makes them ideal for final fits; their teeth are very sharp and cut very quickly. It takes only a very short stroke to get the cut established.

What distinguishes them from most handsaws I've used is that they cut on the pull motion rather than the push. Since the push motion is habitual from growing up with American saws, I found at first that it took a few minutes before I was comfortable enough with the pull motion not to have to think consciously about each stroke.

In recent years thinner blades, which cut thinner kerfs, have been developed for circular saws. Since less material is removed than was taken out by older, thicker blades, the action makes less demand on the saw's motor. Japanese handsaws offer the same advantage. You use less effort than with a standard American handsaw, and you won't tire as quickly.

I haven't used one of my Japanese handsaws long enough for it to need sharpening. I'm not entirely sure that its thin teeth can be sharpened by machine. But these saws aren't terribly expensive, and some of them have a blade that can be discarded and replaced by a new one.

Coping

ONE OF MY reference books describes and illustrates twenty-five different handsaws that a carpenter might use, but only three of them have joined the crosscut saws in my toolbox. For any sawing that involves intricate curves and scrollwork — installing moldings, for example — I use my coping saw. To cope is to cut or shape the end of a molded wood member so that it will cover and fit the contour of an adjoining piece.

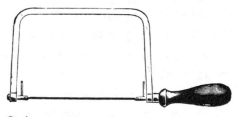

Coping saw

The coping saw has a straight wood handle attached to a looped metal frame shaped like a wide-mouth *U*. A blade only about ⅛ inch wide is fastened between the two open ends of the rigid metal loop and tightened until it has plenty of tension. When the blade gets dull, it can be replaced. Characteristically, blades for a coping saw range from ten to twenty teeth per inch; these are saws for fine work.

What makes the coping saw so flexible is that the blade can be set with the teeth facing whatever direction on a radius of 360 degrees you prefer. The blade can also be installed so that the cutting motion is on the pull stroke (the preference of most carpenters and the one I myself usually elect). Some carpenters reverse the blade so that the cutting motion is on the push stroke, as with a standard crosscut saw. Certain inside cuts can be made with this saw as long as they do not exceed the depth of the *U*-shaped frame (usually about 4½ inches). You bore a hole in what is going to be waste after the cut, insert the detached blade through the hole, attach the blade to the frame, and saw. Because this saw cuts on very tight radii and can replicate curves so well, I find it indispensable for the inside corners of finish molding.

Heavy Metal

THE SECOND SPECIAL saw in my toolbox is a hacksaw, which is designed to cut metal rather than wood. You might wonder about its place in a carpenter's box, but remember that I work with metal fasteners and straps all the time, and occasionally a nail or bolt or screw has to be sawn. The hacksaw is comparable to the coping saw in the way its blade is fastened to the ends of a rigid looping metal frame and then

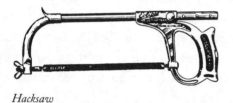

Hacksaw

tightened. But the hacksaw is heavier than a coping saw, and it cuts on the push stroke. One of the best ways to operate a hacksaw is to hold it with both hands — one on the handle, the other on the far end of the frame. With this grip, you can cut the metal with the push stroke, lift the teeth slightly away during the pull stroke, then establish contact again at the beginning of the push stroke. This technique ensures maximum blade performance. Even so, cutting metal is hard on blades. I carry extra hacksaw blades in my toolbox, and as soon as the blade I'm using begins to show dullness I replace it.

Keyhole

SOME PEOPLE CALL it a compass saw, but to me it's a keyhole saw. It has a wood handle like a pistol grip that is attached to a blade about an inch and a quarter at its widest, gradually tapering down to a sharp tip. Don't be fooled by its size. This is a tool for rough-cutting old plaster, plasterboard, plywood, drywall, and most kinds of paneling. I use it more than the other special saws in my toolbox combined. When you need to cut a notch or an opening for a

Keyhole saw

lighting fixture or electrical box in a sheet of drywall, a keyhole saw is the tool to use because you can punch the tip of the blade right through the material to begin the cut. Some of these cuts could be made with a utility knife, but the knife doesn't allow that initial thrust through the material to start the procedure. And some of them could be made with a power drywall cutting tool (a router-like tool with special bits), but not every homeowner or even every carpenter is going to have one handy when he installs a sheet or two of drywall. The keyhole saw is not designed for finish work. It is a nasty, indispensable little weapon for rough carpentry; mine gets pulled out of the toolbox frequently.

Gables

JUST THE OTHER day I installed exterior trim on a garden shed I was building. I wanted the rakeboards to have a nice snug fit where they meet at the top of the gable, and they needed a little shaping to achieve what I had in mind. The traditional tool to trim the ends of the rakeboards is a plane; the high-tech tool is a power circular saw. But both tools would require a trip down the ladder. Happily, I had a crosscut saw within reach, and I knew it could do the trimming I needed.

What you do is tack the boards in place with as good a fit as possible. Then run your handsaw into the joint in a straight vertical cut so that it takes material from the edges of the rakeboards where they fit the tightest. The cut creates a narrow slot as wide as the thickness of the saw's teeth. Now butt the boards together again. If the joint was off quite a bit, you may have to repeat the operation more than once, but eventually you'll get the fit you want.

Other Tight Fits

EXTERIOR AND INTERIOR trim work and other finish carpentry (door and window casings, moldings, rakeboards, stairs, and the like) often require cutting two wood members precisely so they fit together snugly at prescribed angles. Usually the two pieces are supposed to make a 90-degree joint as part of a structure that is square or rectangular, so each piece is cut at 45 degrees. But since the wood is three-dimensional, the cut has to be exactly 45 degrees at one angle and 90 degrees at the opposing angle. It is possible to get the 45-degree angles perfectly cut but to err on the opposing angle to keep the joint square so that the pieces fit in the front but diverge at the back; forcing the joint completely closed will then throw the whole structure out of square.

The miter box is carpentry's answer to the challenge of getting these joints right time after time. The simplest box consists of three pieces of hardwood fastened together to make an upright, square *U*; this structure may have braces across each end of the opening for stability and to counter any tendency of the wood to warp. Matching slots are carefully

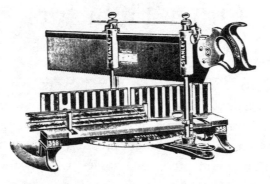

Miter box with backsaw

measured, marked, and cut in the parallel upright legs of the *U* so that a saw coming down through a set of them will make a 90- or 45-degree cut in a piece of wood held inside the *U* tightly against one leg. There will be two sets of 45-degree slots to account for sometimes needing to do 45 degrees angled to the left and sometimes to the right. (If you were building a number of hexagonal picture frames, for instance, you could streamline the measuring and cutting by making a simple miter box with a pair of slots for 60-degree cuts.) I haven't used this kind of homemade miter box very much, but I recall that I did make one to cut moldings on one of my first woodworking shows on television.

Any of three different saws could be used with a simple miter box. The backsaw has a squared-off rather than tapered blade, beveled teeth at a high teeth-per-inch ratio to ensure smooth cuts, and a wood handle like that on a crosscut saw for framing. The tenon saw looks like the backsaw's younger brother, shorter and with even more tpi. Both saws have thin blades with thicker metal spines to prevent buckling. The least likely (but still possible) saw to use for a cut that isn't very deep is a dovetail saw. It has the most tpi of the three and is used for sawing dovetails and other tight joints. Some of the lightweight metal miter boxes sold today have, instead of backsaws with permanent blades, saw frames with thin, replaceable blades to discard instead of sharpening.

Whatever saw you use with a miter box, its condition is of paramount importance: it must be sharp and true. When the metal miter box I carried for years wasn't in use, I kept its backsaw separate, the blade protected by a wood guard tied in place with strings. The saw slid back and forth between vertical guide pins set for any angle between 0 and 90 degrees. The pins kept the saw blade absolutely perpendicular to the piece being cut and tolerated the sawing motion's being slightly off from flat or parallel to the base of the miter box. We are so used to sawing at an angle from the piece to be cut that it takes a conscious mental adjustment to produce the smooth, flat, light strokes needed to cut clean, accurate miter joints.

It wasn't that many years ago that I did all my miter joints with a regular metal box and a backsaw. Now I practically never cut a miter joint by hand. The power miter box took over very swiftly, bringing a new level of sophistication to the job with no financial penalty. (A power miter box doesn't cost more than an excellent hand-operated box.) And the power box can do finer work. A regular miter box in perfect condition can maybe cut to $\frac{1}{32}$ inch, but a power box can get down to $\frac{1}{64}$ inch. In finish work, that's a difference worth considering. Working with a hand-operated box frequently required fine-tuning with a low-angle block plane because it could shave off $\frac{1}{64}$ inch; the power miter box has eliminated final block planing on many miter joints.

The Greatest Invention

"THE INVENTION OF the plane," one of my reference books says, "was the most important advance in the history of woodworking tools in the last two thousand years." A glance at my toolbox appears to refute the claim; planes aren't particularly prominent. Yet I don't for a moment dispute it.

A plane is a deceptively simple instrument that can do three different tasks: shape or size a piece of wood, adjust a piece of wood so that it matches the surface of an adjoining piece, and smooth or finish a piece of wood. All these operations are performed by a single metal blade whose sharp leading edge projects at an angle through a slot in the flat bottom of the tool. When the blade is wedged tightly at the desired angle, the plane can make a uniform impression over and over again as you slide it along a piece of wood.

Theoretically, any of the three tasks could be done with other tools — for example, a wood chisel alone or driven with a hammer. But it would take so much more skill and strength that many operations would be impossibly laborious. The wedged blade of the hand plane leaves both your hands free to guide the tool, a distinct advantage over using a hammer and chisel, and you can lean as much of your weight onto the tool as you want.

When the first planes we know of were used during the Roman Empire, the bodies were often carved from wood and the blade forged of iron, so the blade came to be called an iron. As the plane evolved, you can see that in some way it was inspired by the shape of a human foot, or perhaps a high-top shoe. Or perhaps it was designed without a foot in mind; then the similarity was noticed and enhanced. Regardless, the very obvious physical resemblance of a hand plane to a human foot found a place in the terminology of its parts. The flat bottom is called the sole. The front edge of the body is called the toe. Its back edge, where the handle begins to rise like the line of heel and ankle, is called the heel. The metal sides of most planes rise in a curve about where the arch of the human foot swells.

As with other hand tools, the eighteenth century was a highly inventive period in which the plane grew more sophisticated. The single greatest improvement was the addition of a second metal plate next to the cutting blade. The leading edge of the new metal plate, called the cap, is curved slightly toward the blade. The cap stabilizes the blade and enables it to be thinner than would otherwise be necessary. The cap also interrupts the ribbon of shaving raised by the blade and breaks it off regularly; this reduces the chance that a stroke of the plane will tear out more wood than intended.

Planes began to vary dramatically in size, depending on their specific tasks. A plane designed to remove the waste wood on rough-sawn planks might have a sole at least a foot and a half long; a plane designed for finishing work on a violin case, on the other hand, might have a sole only an inch long and a half-inch wide. I credit R. A. Salaman in his excellent *Dictionary of Woodworking Tools* with mentioning the smallest plane I've seen described in print. He is quoting Francis Young's account, published in London in 1893, that describes how to make a scratch router to carve one or two beads along the edge of a piece of wood. A scratch router is a small block of wood into which a screw is driven until its head is just above the surface, where it serves as a cutter.

Young continues: "'Ah,' says a sharp and clever reader, 'but how are you going to get rid of the rectangular arris left on the other side of the second bead?' Well, this might be a poser to some people, but I should manage it by clearing it off with the cutter of a little toy plane ⅞ inch by ¼ inch that I wear at the end of my watchchain, after the manner of a charm, and which you can buy for the small sum of [one shilling] of Mr. E. Walker, 20, Legge Street, Birmingham." This is the only reference I've found to a working tool used as jewelry. A tie clasp or cufflinks consisting of tiny working planes? The perfect gift for Father's Day or Christmas! I wonder if E. Walker is still in business. In England, it's not impossible.

As planes became specialized, their bodies were frequently made of fine woods such as ebony, rosewood, or boxwood. English planes were seldom embellished, but Continental planes were often beautifully carved. Occasionally, the decoration was superior to the usefulness. Salaman, again, quotes a source who found a handsome rosewood plane — "a most beautiful tool, but it just would not do anything except choke itself after one or two strokes. I lent it from time to time to older craftsmen than myself, but none of them could do anything with it, and I came to the conclusion that it represented some woodworker's experiment, and that he spent so many weeks making it that he could not bring himself to throw it away."

This cautionary anecdote serves as fair warning that the operation of even an effectively designed plane demands more skill and patience than the ordinary use of, say, a claw hammer or a screwdriver. It takes some experimentation to get the knack of planing and quite a lot of practice to be able to pick up a block plane, as a professional carpenter might, and pare down a piece of wood with a few smooth strokes. Virtually anyone can learn to plane well with proper instruction and practice, but along the path to competence are many strokes that end in premature, frustrating chokes.

Plainness Sets In

ABOUT THE MIDDLE of the nineteenth century, planes with steel bodies made their appearance. They are heavier than those with wood bodies — an advantage for some carpenters. The undecided can acquire planes with metal soles and irons but wood bodies. Plain, mass-produced metal planes replaced elaborately decorated ones as the tool became more utilitarian, less elegant. Metal planes were easier than wood models to adapt for special tasks, and their blades or irons could be adjusted and controlled more precisely.

Shortly after the middle of the twentieth century, I started to work with planes myself. Actually, I first played with them, since my Handy Andy toolbox had a small block plane in its inventory. I don't recall using it on the simple projects I built for my sister, but I probably tried to plane the edges of some boards and found it difficult. Or maybe its inherent limits as a tool made for children discouraged me.

When my grandfather retired and moved to Florida, he gave me a small antique wooden tool chest. Among the old tools he'd collected was a metal Stanley molding plane. I still see wooden ones; in fact, some craftsmen continue to make their own, and a few tool catalogues show metal ones. I suppose mine is something of a collector's item now. It has several interchangeable blades, each associated with a conventional molding profile. It also has a guide fence to help keep the plane on track. Older carpenters use these planes to make small pieces of molding for repairs. I doubt that many younger carpenters are even familiar with them. But I remember trying the various blades on odd pieces of wood to see if I could get the right profile to emerge. I had limited success, but it was fun trying. Someday I might even use the plane my grandfather gave me instead of my router-shaper to make a molding for one of my television woodworking projects.

Block plane

When I started working regularly with my father, I carried a block plane, an all-purpose type that many carpenters use for final fitting, finishing, and beveling. Soon I acquired a low-angle block plane, which quickly became (and remains to this day) my all-purpose plane. It is named for its distinguishing feature: the blade is set at an angle of only about 12 degrees from the surface of the sole.

Inventors of the low-angle plane had in mind its suitability for trimming the end grain of wood. When you're planing with the grain, you can safely set the iron at a higher angle so that it bites more deeply into the wood and gets the desired amount of material off the planing surface faster, with less effort. When you're planing across the grain, it's better to shave off material with the blade set at a pretty low angle; otherwise you're apt to chip or gouge the surface.

Low-angle plane

Low-angle planes are ideal for trimming the edges of plywood, particle board, or even plastic laminate as well as the end grain of wood members. Unfortunately, the glue in plywood and composite materials dulls the iron quickly, requiring its frequent sharpening. I like the size of this plane. It slides easily into my toolbelt. It fits my hand comfortably so that I can hold a piece of material with one hand and plane it with my other hand.

My father and I shingled many houses in New England, and I used my low-angle plane to trim the red cedar shingles. Sidewall shingles are applied a little differently than roofing shingles. It is desirable to leave small gaps between roof shingles so they can expand when wet. These shingles are usually not stained or painted, and because they are on a roof, they absorb large amounts of water. Sidewall shingles are laid snugly, but not jammed together. We always bought shingles that were "re-squared and re-butted" — almost perfectly square. But once in a while I would put a shingle up next to its neighbor and the joint wouldn't be snug. I could have shaved them with a regular block plane, since I was planing with the grain of the cedar, but the handy size of the low-angle plane and its flexibility led me to select it for the job.

When I am fitting a miter joint (on a casing for a door or window, for example, or where two rake-boards meet at the peak of a gable) and need to trim one or both surfaces just a little, the low-angle plane proves invaluable. The same is true when I want to back-bevel a board so that it will fit snugly into place where baseboards meet a floor or where they meet in a corner, or when I want to fine-tune the scribed edge of a casing or cabinet stile where it meets a wall.

The reason hand planes have a relatively limited role in my work is simple. The invention of the hand plane was a quantum leap from the hand chisel. Then there was another leap, in our century, from hand to power tools. My hand planes have largely been replaced by power planers, jointers, and surface planers. For the craftsman, the quality of the finished product deserves the highest priority; the next goal is to work as efficiently as possible. There are many situations in which a hand tool is preferable to a power tool, but there are even more situations in which a power tool does an equal or better job in a fraction of the time.

Cousins

THE SMOOTH PLANE is, overall, larger and heavier than a block plane. It is meant to be an all-purpose instrument that a carpenter would use to finish smoothing a surface that he might have rough-planed with an even larger plane. The lumber that most carpenters use today has been milled with more precision than was true when large hand planes were routinely used to shape and trim long boards. But occasionally a board turns up in the materials stack that isn't as straight as I would like it to be, and the smooth plane comes out of my toolbox. I've always carried a smooth plane, but I tell you, that plane has spent more time in the box doing nothing than it has spent earning its keep.

Smooth plane

In practice, you may confirm what I found for myself — that it's far easier to work with a smooth plane when the board is clamped in position, leaving both hands free to operate the plane without fear that the board will shift. At many sites I haven't had a workbench or any other place to clamp boards, so the smooth plane has languished in my box.

The sole of a jointer plane may be as long as 24 inches. It is obviously meant for finishing long pieces of wood. I believe my father carried one, but it has never been part of my toolbox. As I recall, my father used his jointer plane most frequently to bevel the long edges of doors before he replaced it with an electric power plane. The length of the sole is an advantage on a long board, but it also means that there can be significant drag of suction and friction between the surface of the wood and the sole of the plane. Friction is especially apt to develop when the wood being trimmed or smoothed is resinous softwood. The heavier the drag, the more fatiguing it is to operate the plane. Some jointer planes have grooves or corrugations running the length of the sole in order to break up the contact between the sole and the wood being planed, thus reducing the drag.

Rabbet plane

I often make furniture with rabbeted doors, for which I need a rabbet plane. My father was already using this plane when I was a child and he was making cabinets in his basement workshop, but I was an adult before I mastered it. On this plane, the blade or iron is as wide as the sole. In other planes, the slot in the sole through which the blade projects is closed on all sides to give the tool greater strength and to limit the sideways movement of the blade. Consequently, the plane can't get all the way into corners because the blade isn't quite as wide as the sole. But the rabbet plane has a slot that is open at the sides; the blade, therefore, comes right out to the edge of the sole. This plane can slide tightly against a corner with a 90-degree angle.

Suppose, for example, you have an overlay door that was fine when you installed it, but over time the door has swelled and is hitting the stile of the face frame. With a rabbet plane, you can quickly shave one side of the rabbet until the door fits again. Unless you do a fair amount of cabinetmaking, you may have relatively little use for a rabbet plane. But when there is a call for it, no other plane can substitute. The one I own has a blade about ¾ inch wide. One use I make of it is to clean out the bottoms of dados or housed joints that are ¾ inch wide or more. Sometimes, if you cut a dado through a board that isn't perfectly flat, you can't get all of the material out of the middle or, depending on the way the board is cupped, out of the edges. A rabbet plane can remedy the situation quickly if the dado is wide enough to accept the width of the blade.

Plane Tips

PLANES CAN BE tricky to operate, and you can easily ruin a piece of material by rushing into action without testing first. Use scrap material to test the sharpness of the blade, the angle and squareness of the blade, and the kind of trimming or smoothing you want on the real material.

Don't let wood chips accumulate in the mouth of the sole where the blade protrudes.

Make as long, even strokes with the plane as you can. Begin with a little more pressure on the front knob, near the toe, than on the handle, near the heel; then, as you end the stroke, reduce pressure slightly on the knob and apply more pressure on the handle.

Try to begin and end your strokes at the ends of the material you're planing. Try not to begin strokes in the middle of the board because you will leave marks where they begin.

When chamfering corners against the grain of the wood, hold the plane at an angle so that it is shaving down from the top edge.

To reduce the risk of gouging and chipping, plane

in the uphill direction of the grain of the piece of material.

Set the plane down on its side between uses rather than upright on its sole, which could dull the blade.

Resin may adhere to the sole of the plane when you're working on softwood. Don't let it accumulate. Rub any resin off with a rag dipped in a solvent such as turpentine or paint thinner.

The application of a little wax to the sole of a wood plane will make it slide more smoothly on other wood surfaces.

Always retract the blade after use and before storage to prevent its getting chipped during handling.

Store planes by hanging them up or setting them upright on their heels rather than resting on their soles.

Packs of 100

ALTHOUGH I ALWAYS had my choice of two types of utility or mat knife — with either a fixed or retractable blade — I used only a fixed blade for a long time. Not that it didn't have its drawbacks. You could even say that the fixed blade is hazardous because it's almost razor sharp, tapers to a point, and is always sticking out.

Its proper resting place when not in use is blade down in its very own narrow pouch in my nail apron. But there is always the chance that, preoccupied, I might drop it into a wider pouch, reach in there later in search of another tool or a nail, and cut myself. I believe I was generally careful about returning the knife to its rightful place, but the blade was still a problem. Gradually it would wear through the material at the bottom of its pouch and make enough of a hole to drop through until the hole was mended.

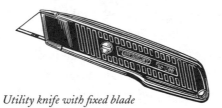

Utility knife with fixed blade

I carry two knives with me: a jackknife, a traditional tool with blades that fold into slots in its handle, and a utility knife, a tool developed in this century to cut common building materials such as drywall and roofing shingles. The latter's metal case is about 5 inches long and fits the hand ingeniously. The blades, which project about an inch from one end of the case, are disposable. Clearly the same inventive mentality gave us the utility knife as gave us the razor with disposable blades, and about the same time.

I was reluctant to adopt the retractable blade because I believed that the mechanism that allowed me to slide the blade out, lock it in place, and retract it again was not reliable. If I pressed too hard against the blade, the mechanism might slip and the blade retract when I didn't want it to — frustrating at best, dangerous at worst. So I chose what I thought was the lesser frustration and hazard: the fixed blade. A tool as simple as the utility knife is subject to improvement, and the mechanism of the retractable blade has been improved to the extent that I now feel confident about its strength.

Usually there is room in the hollow of the case to carry about half a dozen spare blades. Each blade is a trapezoid with a cutting edge at both angled ends. When the first edge dulls, you open the case and turn the blade end for end; when the second edge dulls, you insert a new blade. The blades are not worth sharpening, though I can remember times when my budget was tight and I had run out of blades, so I would run a dull blade over a sharpening stone to get enough of an edge to trim a few shingles. These days I buy blades in packs of a hundred to guard against shortages.

The model I use now has a button I press to open the case instantly, but earlier models were fastened with screws. There often wasn't enough demand for a screwdriver on a framing job to justify carrying one in my toolbelt — except that I needed it for changing the utility knife blade. I solved the problem by taking a nail from my apron and inserting the edge of its head in the groove of the knife's straight slot screw as a makeshift screwdriver. It worked pretty well.

Disposing of used blades can be a nuisance. Blades that are too dull to cut building materials can still cut someone's hand, so I'm leery of throwing them into trash containers as they are. One safe way to do it is to wrap them in pieces of duct tape before discarding.

Let me count the main ways I use my utility knife in framing and other exterior work:

1. Most often, to sharpen marking pencils, particularly octagonal carpenter's pencils, which don't fit conventional pencil sharpeners.
2. To cut rolls of tar paper for the underlayment of roofs or the red rosin paper that we frequently apply under siding. Instead of beginning at one edge to cut across the width of a roll, I stick the point of the knife through the material about an inch from the edge, cut across the width, then return to cut the inch I skipped at the beginning. This technique keeps the roll more stable because the material isn't opening wide behind the blade as you cut.
3. To cut asphalt or fiberglass shingles. You can ex-

tend the life of the blade by cutting on the back of the shingle. If you cut on the face, you expose the blade to the embedded aggregate or stone. You needn't cut all the way through from the back. Score the mark heavily and flex the shingle; it will break cleanly along the score line.

4. To facilitate bending copper or aluminum flashing. If you have to bend a piece of flashing along a line and you don't have a brake (a tool for bending sheets of metal), score a very shallow line and bend the metal over a piece of wood, away from the score. Be careful not to score too deeply because the score makes the metal thinner along that line; the thinner the metal, the sooner it will fail when exposed to the weather.

5. To cut lead flashing to length or to notch it. A sharp blade will cut through lead flashing quite easily.

6. To alter wood shingles. To cut the shingle at the end of a row, overlap it on the one next to it as far as necessary, score it at the overlap, snap off the waste, and trim it — all with your utility knife, doing a final touchup with a block plane, if necessary.

Surgery

I DON'T KNOW many carpenters or tradesmen in general who don't carry a jackknife — not in their toolbox or toolbelt, usually, but in a trouser pocket. This tool should be distinguished, however, from the lighter-duty gentleman's pocketknife or penknife. Its many uses warrant buying a jackknife with a good blade or blades that take and hold a good edge. The main cutting blade should be heavy enough that you can tap its spine with a hammer or mallet when cutting a dowel or other small piece of wood without harming it.

Perhaps a case could be made for carrying a thin jackknife with only one or two blades. I prefer one with several blades, even though it's fatter and heavier. Mine has two cutting blades, one almost the length of the handle, the other shorter. Another blade has a bottle opener and a screwdriver tip. The tips of two of the shorter blades let me use the knife, in the absence of a screwdriver, to turn both Phillips head and straight slot screws. Of the two implements in the ends of the knife, one, a plastic stick like a toothpick, isn't very helpful, but the other, a small pair of tweezers, is very handy in removing slivers or splinters. I won't describe my light surgical techniques in detail but simply note that the tip of my utility knife blade is my field version of the scalpel for gently exposing the end of a splinter enough to grasp it with the jackknife's tweezers.

I prefer to use the very thin blade of a utility knife to sharpen pencils, but my jackknife also does the job well. There isn't any principal task for a jackknife. It nevertheless has a way of coming out of my pocket several times a day — to cut string, open packages, mark (when a pencil isn't handy), score material for bending or breaking, whittle shims, and on and on — but not to play mumblety-peg, which I've outgrown. My jackknife is so much part of my dress for the day that I invariably carry it with me when I travel, and airport security usually doesn't bother me about it.

The Disappearing Tool

SINCE ONE OF my earliest childhood snapshots with a tool showed me holding a screwdriver almost as large as I, you may imagine that screwdrivers have played a central role in my carpentry and woodworking. The truth is: less and less. It's not that I don't drive screws; every week I use one or another size screw to fasten wood members. But I don't use a manual screwdriver.

I don't know of any scientific study, but intuitively one believes the assertion that — contrary to *my* practice — screwdrivers are the most frequently used tools in most homes and shops. The reason is not just that screws are better than nails or other fasteners; screwdrivers are, more than any other tools, used for purposes other than what they are designed for.

Straight slot screwdriver

I'm referring to so-called straight slot screwdrivers, with tips that taper to a flat, squared-off end that fits into a single slot in the head of the screw. They are used as levers to open paint cans — then sometimes to stir the paint! They are used as chisels when a proper wood chisel isn't available or the carpenter is too rushed to fetch one. They are used as scrapers, to remove every adhesive from paint to putty to chewing gum, instead of the scraper blades that would work more efficiently. They are used to pry open an infinite number of stuck items. They are used as punches to pierce or penetrate many different materials. Consequently, you often see screwdrivers with tips that are chipped or rounded off from these renegade uses.

In my first toolbox as a professional carpenter I had an average-size straight slot screwdriver. But even then it didn't get used (or misused) much at all. Carpentry was already switching its allegiance to Phillips head drivers and screws. The shank of the Phillips driver is round and ends in a cross-point that fits into a cruciform depression in the head of a Phillips screw. The conformation of the Phillips driver tip and screwhead gives a better grip than the conventional straight slot. The better the grip, the less force is needed to drive the screw — and the less chance that the screwhead will be stripped by the driver tip.

#2 Phillips head

The three most frequently used Phillips drivers are designated #1, #2, and #3, from smaller to larger. The #1 is used on electrical fixtures or other small jobs. Generally speaking, the only time I need to use a #3 is when I'm driving something like a heavy cap screw into concrete or concrete block or brick. (A cap screw is threaded along its entire length. The ones we use on concrete are referred to as Tap-cons. Driving one requires a considerable amount of force, so the heavy point of the driver and the deep depression in the screwhead are ideal.) My need for a #3 is occasional enough that it doesn't regularly inhabit my toolbox.

But the #2 Phillips driver — that is a tool I couldn't live without. Not as a separate tool, however, with handle, shank, and bit. I've switched almost exclusively to using driver bits chucked in cordless drills. Most tool manufacturers sell screwdriver bits in kits that contain a #1 and #2 Phillips and a couple of straight slot bits. If you look in the drawer where I keep my bits, you'll quickly grasp the whole story. It has many bits, but few, if any, #2 Phillips. Some of the kits have nothing missing but the #2 Phillips. I seem always to be running out of #2 Phillips bits!

A Tool Named Yankee

SINCE THE NINETEENTH century, a number of tool manufacturers in this country have marketed tools under the model or brand name or trademark of Yankee. North Brothers Manufacturing Company of Philadelphia used it to identify its spiral ratchet screwdriver. When the Stanley Works of Connecticut took over North Brothers, it kept the name for the screwdriver that is to this day known simply as the Yankee screwdriver. I believe it can still be purchased. I have a small to medium-size one in my toolbox but rarely use it anymore. However, if I didn't have access to power drivers, the Yankee screwdriver would be my choice.

Tools can be thought of as developing by generations. The Yankee screwdriver is a transition tool, between the regular hand screwdrivers (once called turnscrews) and the power tools I favor today.

Yankee screwdrivers usually have three different settings. The handle and stem can be locked in place, in which case the tool functions as a regular screwdriver. But there wouldn't be any point in having the elaboration of this tool if you used it only in the locked setting. The second setting frees the driver to ratchet a screw, either driving or removing it, like a socket wrench ratchets the head of a bolt. The handle doesn't, however, move up and down on the spiral mechanism.

The third setting adds the force of the spiral mechanism to the ratchet. As the carpenter leans on the handle, the handle remains motionless (that is, it doesn't turn), but the stem pivots and the bit with it, turning the screw. The handle sinks toward the screw as the carpenter pushes it. When a stroke is complete, a spring pushes the handle back out to its position at the beginning of the stroke while maintaining enough pressure on the bit to keep it connected to the screwhead. It is really an ingenious tool. It operates on much the same principle as a power tool, except that a power driver exerts more force than a single carpenter can provide with the weight of his body. There is a further sense in which the Yankee screwdriver is just a primitive version of a power drill. The best Yankee screwdriver comes with interchangeable bits for straight slot and Phillips head screws, and also with a bit to convert it into a spiral ratchet drill.

The Long and Short of It

SCREWDRIVERS COME IN such a variety of sizes and shapes that it's difficult to believe they all belong to the same family. I've seen a picture of a giant straight slot screwdriver that is more than 33 inches long. It wouldn't fit in my toolbox. I'm not sure, holding it by its large fluted handle, that I'd be able to fit the tip into the slot on the screwhead a yard away on the first try.

Toward the other end of the spectrum, I treasure two small screwdrivers in my workshop at home. One has a Phillips head, the other a straight slot tip. At 4 inches, they are far from the shortest screwdrivers made, but they're the smallest ones I need. And they are the tools most easily lost. One can fall out of a toolbox unnoticed. They have an impressive capacity to be hard to find — hiding in corners or under other tools. For the most part I use them on electronic equipment. For example, to remove the clock on my German boiler at home to reset the timing for the heating system, I need a small Phillips head driver; the 4-inch model is perfect for the job.

I could fill most of this book with a treatment of specialized screwdrivers. The kinds I need differ from what I would use as an electrician or plumber or if I worked in the automotive industry or pursued a craft such as jewelry making and repair. Since it is unlikely that I will ever make a coffin as one of my television workshop projects, I guess I won't need the undertaker's screwdriver I've seen illustrated in British toolbooks. It has a very short blade and a flat, oval wood handle.

There are special screwdrivers for gunmakers, pianomakers, and soldier's packs. The latter has three blades with different bits; it looks like what you might get by mating a screwdriver to a Swiss Army knife. One old type of screwdriver that intrigues me is an early-nineteenth-century driver with a long (about 18-inch) flat shank with two indentations called waists because they curve the way a slender person's waist curves.

The shank also has a hole in the base where the carpenter can insert a bar to help turn it, making the screwdriver work on the same principle as a brace bit. One of the human limitations of driving screws by hand is that you have to rotate your hand, wrist, and arm while applying pressure, and the rotating motion affects how much weight can be applied. A turning bar allows you to apply your full weight to the driver while the bar supplies the rotating motion.

Occasionally a special screwdriver will display its variation in the tip rather than in the handle or shank. One screwdriver is designed specifically for assembling billiards tables. Apparently they are held together by many bolts and screws that require great force to drive. Toward the tip of a conventional straight slot screwdriver, the shank widens and flattens and then tapers gently toward the tip. But on the billiards table driver, the shank flares at the end to a tip that is wider than the main part of the shank, making it less likely to slip out of the slot in the bolt or screwhead.

Toolmakers have obviously thought hard about how to design handles for comfort and effectiveness (without always improving things). The handles of the first screwdrivers were turned or carved from wood in a tapered or oval shape to fit the contour of the palm of the hand. Many screwdrivers still retain these shapes and materials. But the most common screwdrivers for home repair and carpentry have tubular plastic handles with fluted indentations to augment your gripping capacity. The question is, how does the handle feel to you when you're exerting maximum pressure to drive a reluctant screw?

One manufacturer offered a screwdriver with a triangular handle, and I found it pretty comfortable. But another brought out a handle with three concave sides that I found uncomfortable, even painful, to grip hard — a perplexing quality to find in a tool designed for professional carpenters.

The material used for the handle makes a difference. On a hot day, smooth wood handles can get pretty slippery from sweat. The fluting of an otherwise smooth plastic handle can help with gripping, but smooth plastic can also get slippery. One screwdriver has a double grip made of textured plastic that would stand up to sweat — or rain — very well. Perhaps the best grip of all comes from handles surfaced with rubber.

I think the search for the perfect grip might be pursued with greater vigor, if for no other reason than as a marketing ploy, except that power tools are now popular even among homeowners for driving screws and bolts. Cordless power screwdrivers have been developed, but I haven't seen many professional carpenters use them. What is more efficient for us is to have screwdriver bits to fit a general-purpose cordless drill.

Think Quality

I HAVE OBSERVED plenty of cheap screwdrivers on the market that wouldn't last long in the hands of a busy carpenter. The tips break or twist because they are made of relatively soft metal. Even the homeowner doing occasional repairs and general maintenance is better served, I believe, by good tools. You should also analyze quality when buying screws. Most wood screws are made of steel plated with a thin coat of zinc. They look good and they're strong, but they offer only modest resistance to corrosion when they're exposed to moisture.

You can also readily find wood screws made of brass or bronze or aluminum. If the head of the screw is going to show, you may want brass or bronze. These nonferrous screws resist corrosion better than regular steel-based screws, but they are made of softer metals, limiting their strength. The material that best combines strength, classy appearance, and high resistance to corrosion is stainless steel. It is more expensive, but I believe the extra money is justified in many applications by its superior qualities.

In my work, as I've said, Phillips head screws account for most of the applications. Straight slot screws are a distant second. Screws with a square indentation in the head, and screwdrivers with a corresponding square tip, have been making their mark — more in woodworking than in general carpentry, I believe — but a square-tipped screwdriver hasn't made it into my toolbox yet. If I worked on my car or television set more often, I might get one of the drivers with a six-point, star-shaped tip to drive the corresponding screws with six indentations around a central spoke. But since I'm always stretching to get my regular projects completed with conventional screws, I leave my car to the mechanic and my television set to the video shop.

Screw Tips

THE QUICKEST WAY to run into problems driving screws is to use a driver and screw that are not well matched. If the tip is too small for the indentation in the screwhead, the driver will twist in place, perhaps chew up the head, perhaps ruin the driver tip; and it will lack the power you need. If the tip is too large, it will mash the head as you exert pressure to force the tip into the indentation. If the tip is wider than the screwhead, it will damage the surface you are driving into when the screwhead is almost flush.

It is usually best to drive a pilot hole with a drill and then drive the screw. If you're using power tools, this is a reason to use a drill with screwdriver bits rather than a power screwdriver. It is easier to change drill bits than to drill pilot holes and then use a power screwdriver. Incidentally, a screw driven into a proper-size pilot hole has more gripping power than one driven directly into the wood. The hole should be about the diameter of the root or core of the screw, without the thread; when the screw is driven into the hole, it only has to displace the wood corresponding to the size of the thread. I have also used a combination tool. The driver bit is chucked in the drill and a twist drill (adjusted for depth) with a countersink slips over the bit. I drill the hole for the screw, slip the twist drill–countersink off, and the driver bit is ready — no need for two power drills or to change bits.

Driving a screw into wood causes friction, which generates heat. The old trick of rubbing some soap or paraffin onto the thread to reduce the friction before driving the screw is as wise as it is old.

If a screw grabs or resists further driving when only partly installed, it is better to back it out of the hole and drill a slightly larger and deeper one than to try to force the screw and risk breaking it off or ruining the head.

In the Plural

A WRENCH HAS two jaws but we refer to it in the singular, as we also refer to a vise or a cutter with two jaws each. Pliers have two jaws and we refer to the tool in the plural — colloquially we even say, "Bring me a pair of pliers," requesting one tool, not two.

There isn't much need in working carpentry for the common pliers found in most households, where they can also substitute for a wrench or vise. Professional carpenters use special kinds of pliers. Of the three types I like to have in my toolbox, the one most like common household pliers is what I call water pump pliers, also known as groove joint pliers. This type has an adjustable jaw, which makes it popular among carpenters. You can also use these pliers to tighten bolts if a wrench isn't handy. Or you can use them for a variety of plumbing jobs. They are handy for disconnecting plumbing fixtures and heating pipes in demolition work.

The smallest type I carry are called needlenose pliers. Their long, tapered grippers remind me of an alligator's jaws. This tool is ideal for pulling things out of tight places. The model I prefer has a cutter built into the base of the jaws, next to the pivot between the jaws and the handle. I use my needlenose pliers when I am working with thin wire, twisting it with the end of the jaws and snipping it with the cutter. Otherwise, they are invaluable for extracting small nails or tacks or brads. I keep in mind, when I use these pliers on electrical wiring or appliances, that the grips do not protect against electrical shock — as, indeed, I keep the same limitation in mind for all my pliers.

Needlenose pliers

Small pliers are designed for use with one hand. For most tasks that this tool is heavy enough to handle, you can grasp them as follows: thumb on the outside of one handle and index finger curving around the same handle; middle and third fingers on the outside of the other handle, and the little finger on the inside of it. This grip allows you to open and close the pliers with one hand. The middle and third fingers exert the gripping power, pulling their handle toward the one anchored by the thumb.

Obviously, this grip is less powerful than one in which all four fingers circle one of the handles, pulling it toward the handle anchored by the thumb. But it is sufficient for the kind of work that needlenose pliers perform. Look at these pliers in a carpenter's or electrician's box and you'll probably find examples with sprung jaws (the jaws don't meet squarely), from twisting material too heavy for the tool to control, or with jaws that don't fully close and cutters that don't meet because of excessive pressure applied to the pivot in work too large for the tool.

Linesman pliers

My largest pliers are called linesman pliers, to acknowledge their indispensability in heavy electrical work. The handles are generally coated with plastic to insulate you from electrical shock should you turn off the wrong circuit (and as long as you're not touching any metal). The cutter is on the outside edge, where the handle meets the jaw. It is strong enough to nip off the end of a 10-penny nail. Ribs on the gripping faces of the jaws allow me to hold metal, wood, and wire surfaces securely. Occasionally I use these pliers when a two-handed grip is most effective.

Jaws

I CAN'T COUNT the number of times I've worked with other carpenters on the first stages of building a house, using their tools, and I've asked, "Got a wrench?" and they say, "No." Many carpenters don't consider the wrench one of their basic tools. Wrenches, they believe, are for plumbers and mechanics. It's true that when I carry both my carpenter's box and my mechanic's box, the wrench and the ratchet with a set of sockets are apt to be in my mechanic's box. But if I carry only a carpenter's box, it contains an 8- or 10-inch adjustable wrench. When a carpenter arrives at the site of a new house, one of the first things he does is bolt the wood sills down to the foundation — hard to do without a wrench.

An adjustable wrench has one fixed and one movable jaw. The gripping surfaces of the jaws may be ridged like teeth or smooth. In my father's and grandfather's days, the type that has been called a monkey wrench since the Civil War was popular. Its upper jaw is fixed, attached perpendicularly to the top of the shaft. As you turn a knurled screw, the lower jaw moves up the shaft until it is tight against the lower side of an object to be turned, or down the shaft, to loosen the jaws after the object has been turned.

A pipe or Stillson wrench is a variation on the monkey wrench. Its lower jaw is fixed to the end of the main part of the shaft. An independent upper shaft, which curves around to form the upper jaw, moves up and down — down to grip the top of the object to be turned, up to loosen — using a screw device between the two shafts similar to the one governing the lower jaw of the monkey wrench. Some of the large pipe wrenches that plumbers use are flexible in the upper jaw to grip pipes better.

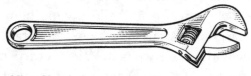

Adjustable 8-inch crescent wrench

The adjustable wrench I carry is called a crescent wrench. Its head has a curved profile. The jaws are at the very top of the head, roughly aligned with the shaft, and the thumbscrew adjustment is set into the head, close to perpendicular to the shaft. This placement of the jaws gives you better leverage than the older monkey wrench.

Every carpenter has handled wrenches that have

loosened up after long use. The movable jaw goes slack so that it doesn't stay quite parallel to the fixed jaw; the greater the play, the less effective the tool is.

Pipe wrench

Carpentry requires an increasing variety of metal fasteners. A typical day's work may include installing some joist hangers or attaching wood members with lag bolts or through bolts. It's very time-consuming to apply an adjustable wrench to many of these fasteners. I prefer to use a ratchet with interchangeable sockets. If you buy a mechanic's box that includes a kit of tools, you will probably find that it has a greater variety of sockets than you usually need. In ordinary house construction, the bolts commonly used can be installed with sockets ranging from ⅜ to ¾ inch. Any socket beyond that range is going to stay in the toolbox most of the time. Thus, if I want to put a few mechanical tools in my carpenter's box, I'll make a place for one adjustable wrench and a ratchet with just a couple of sockets. There's no point in carrying tools seldom used.

Reality Check

Brewer's Dictionary of Phrase & Fable sheds no light on the origins of the phrase "hard as nails," but it says the term has both a physical and a figurative sense — physical as in a man of splendid fitness being hard as nails. I can't recall ever hearing a carpenter refer to anything structural as being hard as nails. It is the figurative sense I'm familiar with — of being temperamentally harsh, unfeeling, unsentimental — and I've heard it applied more often to certain types of women than to men. Beware, she is hard as nails. Or is it that men as a class are assumed to be hard as nails and women not to be, but some are?

Rest easy. Nails actually are far from the hardest things in the world. If you drive one with a misdirected hammer stroke, it will bend over in the most frustrating way. According to a book I once saw, real men don't eat quiche. That's debatable, but I'm willing to stand by the view that real carpenters don't leave mishit nails in wood (or try to flatten them sideways against the surface before starting again with another nail). The framers who worked on my house a couple of years ago reminisced about contractors whose foremen would send them home for the day (without pay) if they found them leaving mishit nails in the frame. Real carpenters pull and discard the cripples.

Not the Wrist, Doc

HAMMERS REFLECT THE terminology of the head as notably as wood planes imitate the shape and terminology of the human foot. The entire metal structure at the striking end of the hammer is called a head. The flat or slightly convex surface, used to strike a nail or other object, is its face, which is also sometimes slightly rounded off or chamfered at the edge. Behind the face is a barrel-shaped segment called the bell (a departure from organic metaphors), but the remainder of the head from the bell back to the midsection, where head and handle intersect, is called the neck and has a concave shape that looks like a human neck.

The antecedents of the hammers I use today had wood handles anchored in a hole passing through the middle of the head. Where the handle showed on the top of the head was known as the eye, since it was often oval, and the flattened sides of the metal midsection, parallel to the face, were the cheeks.

These names are apt. Just as the eye and cheeks of a human face are vulnerable to injury, to shattering, the eye and cheeks of the hammer are the thinnest parts of the handle and head, respectively, and therefore prone to injury; they are close to the point of impact and shock when the hammer strikes true and frequently absorb the blow directly in a mishit. If you've seen a variety of old hammers, you've noticed that some have extra wedges or nails driven into the eye to tighten the fit, and you've seen some with splits like old bone breaks apparent in the handle at the eye. Hammers take lots of punishment. The least you can do, therefore, is strike only with the face. Don't swing a hammer sideways so the cheek, which is the weakest part of the head, takes the blow directly.

The other half of the hammer's head, from the midsection to the end opposite the face, is called the peen. There are scores of different shapes of hammer heads, particularly of the peens. Some peens are semispherical (ball peens); others are tapered to a point like a cold chisel blade — with the edge perpendicular to the handle (cross peen) or parallel to it (straight peen). Many of the peen variations are related to the needs of specific trades. One curious and delicate English pair, called the Gentlemen's and Ladies' hammers, are similar to an upholsterer's hammer. The peen is a claw with a *V*-notch for pulling nails. The Gentlemen's claw comes straight back from the midsection, and the Ladies' claw is curved — regarding which R. A. Salaman notes wryly, "It would be hard to say what this difference implies." (Is the lady who uses one of these disposed to be hard as nails?)

In trade journals these days you can find articles about medical research into what types of handle design and material best combat fatigue or injuries to the wrist and arm from repetitive hammering. If typists can fall prey to carpal tunnel syndrome or other chronic injuries from striking their keyboards, it stands to reason that carpenters, who hammer with much greater force day after day, might be doing something harmful to their bodies. The tests always show that the worst offender is the kind of hammer I have used for decades, a hammer with a head and handle made of one continuous piece of steel. Fiberglass handles are alleged to be the next worst offender because they bounce quite a lot. Wood handles get positive ratings because the wood absorbs much of the shock from each blow.

If I were doing medical research to help carpenters, however, I wouldn't emphasize the wrists and arms. It's the back and knees you have to worry about first. Every day a carpenter lifts and holds materials at awkward angles, stands on ladders and joists for long periods of time, kneels on unforgiving surfaces, stresses his body in countless ways. I've been lucky not to have back problems and my knees are still pretty

[151]

good, but I believe these are the main places where carpenters' bodies come to grief. I've never experienced any pain or problems with my wrists or arms. I don't remember the actual lesson, but someone, probably my father, taught me at an early age that the proper way to swing a hammer is with the whole arm, not from the wrist; if you follow this principle, I think it will save stress on your wrist and forearm, too.

Weightlifting

THERE WAS A hammer in my Handy Andy toolbox, but I don't remember paying as much attention to it as to some of the other tools. When I began working with my father, I carried a 20-ounce hammer and used it for both framing and finish carpentry, as he did. The practice of many carpenters at that time was to carry two claw hammers: a 20-ounce model for framing and a 16-ounce one for finish work. They both were 13 or 13-plus inches long. You could get a standard nail hammer as light as 13 ounces, but that weight is better suited to home repair than framing or even finish carpentry.

I don't remember seeing any carpenters at that time using hammers heavier than 20 ounces. The heavier (22-ounce), long-handled (16½-inch) framing hammers weren't in general use then. The issue of a hammer's weight and length of handle is a judgment call each carpenter makes. The heavier the hammer and the longer the handle, the more force it exerts in a typical strike; or, the lighter the hammer and shorter the handle, the harder you have to strike to get the same result. Since you're carrying it on your toolbelt all day and probably striking with it hundreds of times, you want it to be as light as feasible.

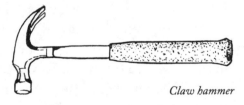

Claw hammer

The judgment my dad and I made was that the 16-ounce hammer is too light for framing, but, used carefully, the 20-ounce is fine for finish work and saves the bother of toting two hammers. In recent years I've spent more time making projects in my workshop than framing houses. When a friend gave me a 16-ounce hammer, I began using it regularly because it's a better weight than 20 ounces for shop work, but my 20-ounce hammer is still in my toolbox, ready for the next framing assignment.

For the better part of my carpentry career, I've used hammers with padded handles made of leather wrapped around the steel shaft in parallel strips. Personally, I like a padded handle. It's easy on the hands, and it doesn't get slippery from sweat in hot weather the way a bare wood handle can. (One way to make a hardwood handle less slippery is to sand off the finish where you grip it with coarse sandpaper.) If a handle is covered with a softer material than hardwood that has some give to it, it will gradually wear and take on the contour of your grip.

Tradesmen differ on their preference for the shape of the claw. I like a curved claw for its ease in removing nails and because I think it is slightly less liable to injure me or someone else. I've seen carpenters take too long a backstroke and hit themselves or someone close to them. It is better to get struck with the curve of a claw than with its sharp beveled tip.

Roofers are among those who often carry hammers with straight, or ripping, claws. There is a little arc in the peen of these hammers, but they look straight next to a curved claw. If a roofer loses his footing and starts sliding toward a fall, he can flip his hammer around and drive the claw into the roof to check himself — much as a mountain climber drives his pick into an icy slope to stop a slide.

Some carpenters claim you can get more leverage pulling nails with a straight than with a curved claw.

When I was first hiring out as a carpenter (and not as strong as I am now), I quickly learned how much more leverage you can get pulling a seemingly intractable nail by putting a small block of wood under the claw before you pull. The difference is incredible.

There is no mystery about hammering. The longer the stroke and the closer to the end of the handle the hammer is grasped, the more power it delivers. People who don't practice regularly are understandably cautious: they grip up on the handle, use their wrist rather than their whole arm, and shorten their stroke, gaining more control but forfeiting power. Baseball players follow the same principle; some of them shorten their grip on the bat to improve their accuracy in hitting, but they sacrifice a lot of power.

It's not as difficult as you might think to actually hit the nail on the head. Of course, the action is affected by the degree of eye-hand coordination you have naturally. But the key is to focus carefully on the nailhead during the entire stroke. Then you won't find hammering frustrating even while gripping the base of the handle and taking a full stroke.

Don't Reduce the Fractions

IN FINISH CARPENTRY, you often use a nail set in conjunction with your hammer. In framing it suffices to hammer the nails flush with the surface or slightly below because you don't care if the hammer face mars the surface of the stud or other framing member in the final strokes. What is a matter of indifference in framing becomes vital in finish work. You usually want to drive finish nailheads a little below the surface so you can fill the indentation with woodfiller and make the nail disappear with no marring of the wood as a telltale sign.

Just before the finish nailhead reaches the surface, therefore, you put a nail set — a steel pin about 4 inches long — between hammer and nail. The first ¾ inch of the end you strike is square, but the edges of the striking face are rounded off a little, or chamfered, to lessen the risk that a mishit will chip a fragment off. The midsection is cylindrical, about 1¾ inches long; it has a textured surface to make it easier to grip. The end placed on the nailhead is a slender cone, tapering down to a tip intended to fit certain sizes of finish nails. The heads of finish nails have a slight depression in the middle to help keep a nail set in place, and the tip of the nail set has a depression in the middle as well, to help keep it from slipping off.

Nail sets are identified by the diameter of the tip. The most common ones begin at $\frac{1}{32}$ inch and progress by increments of $\frac{1}{32}$ inch up to $\frac{5}{32}$ inch. We've all been so conditioned to reduce fractions that I automatically refer to $\frac{2}{32}$ as $\frac{1}{16}$ and to $\frac{4}{32}$ as $\frac{1}{8}$, but the nail sets themselves are marked only in x/32s. My dad carried three: $\frac{2}{32}$, $\frac{3}{32}$, and $\frac{4}{32}$. You soon learn the size nails they really fit. Theoretically, they're supposed to match on the job. You see what size finish nail you're about to drive, select the proper nail set from your apron, and proceed. As my grandchildren would say, "Not." The truth is, you seldom have the exact size you need. I make do by carrying a small nail set, a $\frac{1}{32}$ or $\frac{2}{32}$, and a midsize, a $\frac{3}{32}$ or $\frac{4}{32}$. It's better to have a nail set that's a little too small than one that's too big for the nailhead. In a pinch, I make do with a 16-penny common spike — I slightly flatten the point before driving another nail with it.

If the nail set is the smallest of my hammering tools, my sledgehammer is the largest. It's surprising how often I use it. Obviously the sledge is essential in taking walls down, but its construction applications are equally important. When I raise an interior partition frame that I've laid out and fastened together on the deck, there's a point in the raising, just before the frame is fully vertical and in place, that is very tight, and I need a heavy pounder to drive it into place. My 6- or 8-pound sledge (32 inches long with an ash handle) has the oomph I need.

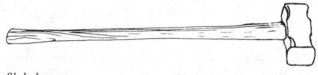

Sledgehammer

The sledge also comes in handy when I'm installing tongue-and-groove plywood subflooring. The joints have to be driven together, but hitting the edge of a sheet directly with a sledge would damage the wood. I put a 2-by-4 on edge against the plywood and strike the board with the sledge.

I remember one time at the end of the day when a fellow carpenter — I believe he was framing a window — playfully tried to drive a number of nails with a single blow of a sledge. On paper it looks efficient. One swing, if accurate. But even the relatively light sledge I use would seem awfully heavy at the end of a day if I used only it for nailing.

There's what amounts to a smaller version of a

sledgehammer, weighing in at 3 pounds with an overall length of about 16 inches. Masons sometimes use these 3-pounders to break stones. They're also good for driving cold chisels or driving stakes into the ground. If you're building a retaining wall with heavy, pressure-treated wood fastened with 60-penny spikes, you'll find this driver the ideal tool.

I've used a mason's hammer from time to time, but not often enough to exhibit the touch of a good mason. It is designed to score and break brick and cement block. With experience, you can score a line with the peen end where you want to break a brick or block, causing a fracture point, then knock off the waste piece with a crisp blow so that it breaks along the line. The striking face is square rather than round, like a conventional nail hammer face, and the peen is unusually long, tapered to a fairly sharp chisel edge. The tool is also known as a prospector's pick or hammer and has been seen in countless Westerns.

A ball peen hammer is usually considered part of a mechanic's repertory rather than a carpenter's, but I work with rivets on gutters and other metalwork often enough that I have to know how to "peen" or flatten them. The identifying characteristic of this hammer is the dome of the peen. I don't need it often enough to justify always carrying one in my toolbox, but it gets added to the mix if there is any chance I'll be working around sheet metal on a given day.

Toenails

A HAMMER THAT has been used for a long time may have a face so worn and rounded that it easily slips off nails unless the strike is very close to true (many strikes vary somewhat from true but don't knock the nail off course). There isn't much to be done about it except admit it's time for a new hammer. But hammer faces may also slip because enough of the coating on some nails has rubbed off and built up on the face to make it slippery. There *is* something to do about it: sand the face with fairly coarse (100- or 80-grit) sandpaper.

We associate nailing mainly with driving a nail straight through one piece of material into another. But carpentry, both rough and finish, often compels you to toenail: to drive a nail at an angle other than 90 degrees to the plane of the surface being nailed. It takes some practice to get the hang of it.

Framers, to give an example, have to do a lot of toenailing while fastening studs one at a time down onto sill plates or up onto top plates. The fastening might be done with two nails on one side of the stud or with two on one side and one on the opposite side. You start the nail in the stud about ¾ inch back from where the stud and plate intersect, nailing at an angle of about 45 degrees. If the angle is too great, the hammer blows will tend to push the end of the stud off its intended position. If the angle is too small, the nail may split the wood you're nailing it into. As you drive the nail, the head gets close to the surface of the wood well before the shank is fully driven. At that point, you have to adjust your strikes so that you're hitting the nailhead toward the edge of your hammer face rather than dead center. You may have to do this while hammering from an awkward position — above your head, for example. Yet with practice you will find it manageable. Professional carpenters have toenailed so many times that they make the adjustments in their strokes without thinking.

There's another situation that calls for nailing at an angle. Let's say you're making a window header by doubling studs, and one stud is not completely flush with the other. You can pound the one you want to move until it's in the right place, but it will likely bounce back rather than stay put. One solution is to drive a nail at an angle through the one you want to move and into the other piece. When they're tight, keep driving; the angled nail will pull the first piece a little into alignment and hold it there. Again, practice will show you what nail angle will give you a specific amount of adjustment.

One of your concerns when driving finish nails is

that the nail not split the wood and ruin the piece. What I do is turn the nail end for end, place the head where I'm going to drive the nail, and give the pointed end a tap with my hammer. This converts the wedge-shaped tip into a flat end that pushes the wood ahead of it rather than forcing the wood apart. I think (but can't prove) that this technique compresses the wood fibers a little where I'm going to drive the nail and makes them less likely to break apart. What I know is that this trick works for me every time.

My final thought about hammers is to underline the cautionary advice printed on many hammers when you buy them. Wear safety glasses or goggles when hammering, particularly when striking another metal tool such as a cold chisel or pry bar. Nails don't splinter very much, but they may fly when the first strike is off-center. But other tools may shed sharp fragments of metal when struck, and wood or other material may send splinters flying.

Barhopping

UNLESS SOMEONE HAS grievously misread a set of architectural or engineering specifications, carpentry in new construction doesn't often require taking things apart on a big scale. But a major segment of residential construction involves renovating, rehabbing, or adding on to existing buildings. We are constitutionally restless with our homes; we can't leave them alone. When we buy an existing house and move into it, we are apt to renovate sooner or later to make it further approximate the house of our dreams. A new fashion in kitchens or bathrooms or family rooms strikes, and we call in the contractors. If we're going to enlarge the kitchen, why not create a masterful bedroom and bath above it at the same time?

When a carpenter has to rip out walls, floors, and ceilings, his pry bars come out of the toolbox. There are other occasions — for example, taking down temporary scaffolding — when bars are invaluable during new construction for removing nails and wrenching boards and braces apart, but demolition gives bars their longest, hardest workouts.

Working end of crowbar

The first bar I learned to use was a Cat's Paw. Basically, it's a forged steel nail puller. Most types of bars are made in a number of sizes. The hexagonal handle of mine was relatively short, about 8 to 9 inches long; it curved 90 degrees at one end into a claw: a tapering down of both width and thickness into a narrow pointed end from which a *V*-notch was cut. The claw was much like the one on a claw hammer except that it was more pointed, because it was going to be used frequently to dig into wood to snag a nailhead that was flush with or below the surface. I'm not sure how the tool came to be called a Cat's Paw. The curved neck, rounded on the outside like the curve of a spoon, and tapered claw make it look more like a snake's or duck's head (with a notch in the bill) to me.

You should start removing a nail with the claw about ¼ inch away from the head, pushing or driving it down and forward until the nailhead is caught in the notch; then the handle and claw operate like a claw hammer to lever the nail out. (Carpenters often will use their Cat's Paw to raise the nailhead enough to snag it with their claw hammer to complete the removal.) If the nail is flush with or below the surface, you may have to drive the claw into the wood a little to catch the head. The neck is bent to make it easy to drive the claw forward by striking the neck with a hammer. Start driving the claw at about 45 degrees to the surface, and reduce the angle by pulling the handle more vertical to the surface as you get beneath the nailhead.

I've seen carpenters need a Cat's Paw to dig out a nail but not want to take the time to get one from their toolbox, so they borrow another worker's hammer and use its claw as a makeshift Cat's Paw, driving it by hitting its striking face opposite the claw with their own hammer. I don't recommend this practice at all.

On occasion, you may be pulling a nail with a claw hammer and the nailhead breaks off, leaving the shank embedded in the wood. Sometimes you have maneuvering room to bend the shank far enough over with a sideways motion of the hammer claw to grip the shank and pull it, but if the claw is worn you may not be successful. The Cat's Paw may work where the hammer failed to catch the shank in its sharper notch or to bend it sideways enough to grip it.

In most instances, you can't remove a nail with a Cat's Paw without marring the surface of the wood, so it's meant to be used for demolition and rough framing, where the wood is to be discarded or covered with other material. However, I've seen a Cat's Paw for furniture makers that shows how a rough-and-tough tool can be refined almost to elegance. The claw is much more delicate, and the opposite end of the handle has been machined into a wafer-thin blade for inserting between and easing apart adjacent surfaces.

The end of the handle opposite the claw on my first Cat's Paw had not been machined to use as a tool. Most of the ones I've seen on jobs look like that. But I have used Cat's Paws that had claws on both ends (one turning 90 degrees, the other flaring out gently about 30 degrees from the axis of the handle), though I don't see any great benefit to be gained from the second claw except that it lengthens the tool slightly, and every inch of length adds to its leverage. I have also seen them with a straight prying blade, like that of a cold chisel, on the end opposite the claw.

Right Between the Eyes

I SUSPECT THAT almost everyone who does much carpentry or home repair has been guilty of the error I'm about to describe. This is how I learned the hard way not to do it again. It happened on Nantucket, where I also had a mishap with my framing square. I was up on a stepladder, pulling something apart with my flat bar, when I was called away to look at something else on the project. When I returned, I grabbed the ladder to move it to a slightly different location before climbing it again.

Just as I started to tip the ladder back from the framing, I remembered that I had left my bar on the top step of the ladder (first mistake), and the act of remembering made me instinctively look up (second mistake). The bar hit me square on the forehead. A flat bar in freefall does not tickle. Fortunately, it was the blunter end that struck me; if it had been the sharper edge it might have gashed me, even injured an eye. There's a special temptation to put down tools that don't fit in your toolbelt, leaving them where they can be dislodged even by the jarring caused by others working nearby. Haste or carelessness can make us leave even tools that we ordinarily secure in our toolbelts lying around where they can injure someone else if they drop. You feel bad enough when the error injures only yourself; you feel worse when it injures someone else.

Teardrops

THE FLAT BAR is a pry bar used principally to separate wood members from one another; it is only secondarily a nail puller. The early ones I was familiar with had heavy round or hexagonal metal handles, about 14 to 16 inches long, that tapered at one end into a flat blade with a nail-pulling slot in the middle. The blade was not as sharp as a chisel's, but it could be driven into the seam between two boards. When I wanted to separate two studs that were nailed together, I drove the flat bar blade between them where I knew or thought the nails would be until I got them into the notch in the middle of the blade's end; then I drove the blade a little farther until it sheared off the nails.

A few inches up the handle from the edge of the blade was a teardrop opening. If you worked a board loose enough that its nails popped up a little, you could drop the wider part of the teardrop down over them, move the bar enough to snag the nailheads securely at the narrowest part of the teardrop, and pull them.

The flat bars usually seen today are like the second one I got for myself. They have tapered or beveled blades on both ends, and the entire length of the tool is a ribbon of steel, which in my model is about 1⅜ inches wide and ¼ inch thick. One of the blades flares just about 30 degrees, and the other, like the curved end of the Cat's Paw, bends around 90 degrees from the shaft. You can pound the neck of this second end to drive the sharply tapered, notched blade between two boards to get prying leverage. At least some of these bars aren't quite as flat as their name implies. The metal stock they're made of is very slightly curved crosswise, which I believe makes the bar stronger.

Many flat bars made today are of lighter steel, which has more flex than the early bars. I've used both, but I've never lost my preference for the older, heavier version with less flex. When I'm prying up planks, I don't want the bar to bend. Still, the flexible flat bars have their advocates when it comes to replacing clapboards.

The relative thinness of the shaft and blade allows you to drive the blade at the flat end carefully under a damaged clapboard so that the notch intersects the nail, and a little prying makes the nail pop up. But clapboards can be tricky. Sometimes, after you ease the bar out from under the clapboard, the nail goes back into its hole enough so that you can't get a claw under the head to pull it. After you have loosened the board and nail with the first insertion of the bar, take your hammer, slide the claw under the clapboard, and hold the board out from the sheathing far enough to release the pressure on the bar. Reposition the bar as close to the wall as possible and push the notch against the nail firmly enough that the nail can't move (if you're lucky, the bar will slide right under the tip of the nail, blocking it from going back into the hole). Release the hammer's hold on the clapboard; it will spring back toward the sheathing enough to expose the nailhead to the claw of your hammer.

Just as there is a refined version of the Cat's Paw for making furniture, so there is a small version of the flat bar, available in a nickel-plated finish over tempered steel. It has both the 30- and the 90-degree notched end blades and a little teardrop in its 7 inches of length. Finish carpenters value this model for its ability to slide under or between moldings or other bits of trim, which can then be pried off without doing much damage to them.

Another tool, incidentally, that is good for removing interior wood trim is a putty knife. My father, who didn't carry one of the 7-inch flat bars, always kept one in the tray of his toolbox. The thin blade, which slides pretty easily even under painted trim, is stiff enough to loosen the smaller finish nails.

Ripping bar

For heavier work than a flat bar is designed for, I turn to my ripping bar. Its shaft is hexagonal, like the handle of a Cat's Paw, and it curves about 120 degrees at one end like a swan's neck to a notched point that is ideal for pulling heavy nails. The opposite end is angled slightly from the shaft and tapered to an edge that can be driven between heavy planks. I've seen rippers in lengths from 2 to 4 feet, and I used to have a 4-footer, but the shorter ones are more common.

The long, heavy handle gives you the leverage you need to pry up boards.

(I should mention here that bars in general are made of steel of varying quality. The longer the bar, the more stress you are going to put on the metal as you apply leverage. Bars of lesser-quality steel will break on occasion; those of high-grade steel last a lifetime.)

The applications of bars to new construction are as important as, if less frequent than, their use in demolition. You might, for example, have a board that isn't perfectly straight that you want to nail to rafter tails as a fascia. If the curvature isn't too pronounced, you can nail each end, then straighten it into place at other points, using the leverage of your ripping bar, and nail it before releasing the bar.

Laborers need crowbars more than carpenters do, but carpenters as well as homeowners occasionally have to dig holes for a little footing or for the foundation pier of a deck. Nature usually contrives to bury at least one large stone just where you want to make a hole. The long (5- to 6-foot) shaft and slightly flattened tip of the crowbar allow you to work around and raise a buried stone or break up compacted soil or do any task that requires maximum manual leverage.

The last bar I carry with me is quite odd and appears to be a hybrid of several of the others. If anything, it slightly resembles the thin blades used to slide down car windows to release locks when the keys have been locked inside.

The bar begins with a hexagonal steel handle about as long as that of the simplest Cat's Paw — about 8 inches. The handle then bends almost at a 90-degree angle for about 2 inches to create a neck that keeps the handle comfortably above the plane of the blade and, more important, provides a surface to strike while using the bar. The bar bends again, away from but roughly parallel to the plane of the handle, but now it has flattened out to look like a 1¼-inch-wide flat bar. The top side, with slightly chamfered edges, runs along for 16 or 17 inches to a straight tapered edge almost 1¾ inches wide. A tail comes back from each side of the tapered edge to form a deep *V*-notch with its side of the flat bar. Not a notch for pushing forward to catch nailheads, but a notch facing back toward the handle.

The bar is a shingle ripper. The challenge of removing a single shingle is that the nails holding it to the roof underlayment or side wall are blind, covered by overlapping shingle courses. It helps to know that shingles are held in place by two nails, each about ½ inch in from the long side and about ½ to 1 inch above the butt end of the overlapping shingle. Because of the overlapping installation, a single shingle may be penetrated by two sets of nails: its own and a set from the next overlapping course.

Slide the bar under a defective shingle and work it forward until you have passed the nails fastening it to the roof or siding underlayment, tapping the 2-inch neck forward with a hammer, if necessary. Catch the nails in one of the notches as you pull the shingle bar back (striking the neck in the opposite direction), pulling them loose with the shingle or, just as likely, shearing them off. Now the shingle can be removed without damaging the surrounding ones and a new one slipped into place. You can see this is a very useful tool. Some shinglers today choose to slide a power reciprocating saw blade underneath a defective shingle to shear off the nails, but I believe this is an instance of the hand tool, the shingle bar, being the ideal instrument for the job.

Cuts and Bruises

MANY CARPENTERS CARRY a fairly heavy wood chisel as a secondary pry bar; it is not as finely honed as a chisel used for mortising. I carry one for occasional roughing out. It becomes a prying tool with the advantage that it's easier to drive into wood than the tapered or beveled edges of my other bars. You need to be careful when using a tool with a relatively sharp edge, like a pry bar; if it slips, it can cut you worse than a regular bar blade. A tool like my secondary chisel, which is meant to be very sharp, like a wood chisel, but is deliberately kept a little dull, is as dangerous as a very sharp tool.

True Chiselers, Mere Cheats

WORDSMITHS CAN TRACE the many variants of chisel, the English noun and verb signifying a hand tool and its use, back at least six hundred years, but its colloquial and slang origins, meaning to cheat or defraud, are both more recent and quite obscure. One day a chisel was an honorable tool; the next, it was also a sin.

Woodworkers have used this tool in one form or another since Neolithic times. Traditionally, a chisel had two parts: a metal blade with the cutting end ground to a sharp edge, and a handle, usually of wood. Sometimes the two parts were joined by inserting the pointed end (opposite the cutting end), or "tang," of the blade into a hollow in the handle; other times the tapered end, or "socket," of the handle was inserted into the hollowed end of the blade. Where the two parts met, a leather washer was often added to absorb some of the shock when the chisel was struck with a mallet; the same purpose was also accomplished by fastening a leather tip to the pounding end of the handle.

Wood chisel

As I mentioned earlier, I've always carried my wood chisels in a canvas pouch my mother made so that each chisel has its own slot. The chisels in my carpenter's box are meant for general carpentry rather than the finest aspects of cabinetmaking. They have plastic handles, which some authorities criticize because a shattered handle renders the tool useless while a broken wood handle can be replaced, but I think the plastic handles stand up well to the demands of general carpentry. A metal cap on the end of the handle allows the chisel to be struck with a hammer instead of a mallet. (Whenever metal strikes metal, there is always a risk that a sharp fragment will break off and take flight, so I always wear safety glasses or goggles when I strike my wood chisels with a hammer.)

The cutting end of every chisel is beveled, of course. One side of the blade may be beveled along the edges as well or both sides may be straight. Straight-sided chisels are probably a little stronger, but I prefer having the beveled side. It comes down to which shape you find more comfortable, especially in situations where you are pushing the chisel rather than driving it with a hammer, grasping the handle with one hand and guiding the blade close to its cutting edge with the other thumb and fingers.

I find it best to carry a set of six wood chisels with blades in widths that begin at ¼ inch and increase by ¼-inch increments up to the widest at 1½ inches. Two of them, the ¾- and 1-inch, get used far more than the rest of them combined. The 1-inch blade is the best for chiseling out the space for strike plates on doorjambs. The ¾-inch blade is ideal for squaring up dados when building cabinets, since I frequently use ¾-inch stock. Generally speaking, I use the other chisels for mortising hinges, locks, and doors — for the finish carpentry aspects of construction and renovation.

Becoming skillful with a chisel simply takes a lot of practice and familiarity with techniques that improve the chances a job will turn out as you hope. For example, if you need to mortise out a latchplate in the edge of a door, you have to remove the wood neatly and to a uniform depth, squared off, within a specific outline. First you score the outline of the plate with a utility knife. Then you make several crosscuts ⅛ to ¼ inch apart with the chisel perpendicular to the wood and across the grain, trying to strike with the same force each time so the crosscuts have the same depth. Holding the chisel at a low angle with the cutting edge parallel to the crosscuts, you chisel with the grain to remove a layer of material, level off any unevenness, and square off the corners and sides, using both taps with a hammer and hand chiseling as the situation suggests. You repeat this process, if necessary, until the mortise is the right depth to let the plate sit perfectly flush with the surface of the door. The point of removing uniform thin layers is to avoid cutting the mortise so deep that the plate sits below the surface of the surrounding wood — a problem for which there is no elegant solution.

Cold chisel

In addition to my wood chisels, I also carry a cold chisel. Its pounding surface, shaft, and blade are one continuous piece of hard steel. Wood chisels are reasonably tough, but they're not pry bars. If you drive one too hard, you may snap the blade or the handle. You can chip the cutting edge of a cold chisel, but I've never heard of anyone snapping off the blade or handle. The cutting edge is tapered on both sides (rather than beveled on one side like a wood chisel), and it isn't very sharp. It doesn't need to be. I use mine largely for chipping concrete or concrete block around new foundations and piers for decks.

Whose Best Friend?

WHEN I PUT together my first toolbox, I included a small rectangular oilstone. It came in its own box and had a coarse grit on one side, a fine grit on the other. To sharpen an edge, I put a little oil on the sharpening surface I wanted and then worked the blade against the stone with a circular motion and at the proper angle for the tool. A few minutes' attention to the edge of a chisel or a plane blade or even a jackknife blade worked wonders on its effectiveness. Dull blades exact a double penalty. They make you work harder, yet the results are still inferior.

My father was very good at sharpening tools freehand. If a chisel was badly nicked, he would first even it out against a grindstone — a heavy disk cranked by hand or powered by a motor — then do the fine-tuning with an oilstone. He could produce a bevel so even it looked machined.

The trick is to sharpen the edge at the angle that is right for the tool. For those of us who lack my father's eye and experience, toolmakers have come up with calibrated jigs or templates that hold the blade consistently at the right angle to the sharpening surface. They're inexpensive, and they really work.

Oilstone in a box

When I talk with Tedd Benson in New Hampshire about the sharpening techniques his crews use in timberframing, I see how sophisticated this art can be. Joinery is central to his structures, and a dull tool is more than a nuisance when fashioning mortise-and-tenon joints, which have to fit perfectly; it's a disaster. So Tedd uses an impressive array of Japanese waterstones.

In my kind of carpentry, the oilstone is adequate for most purposes, and I would still be using one today except that it has been superseded. Not long ago, a stone was introduced with a plastic core under a metal plate impregnated with industrial diamonds. Who would have thought diamonds are a carpenter's best friend?

Diamond stones come in various grades of coarseness and fineness, often coded by color. Only one side of the stone is a sharpening surface, so you have to carry two or three stones rather than one. The diamond surface sharpens faster and better than the oilstone, however, and its lubricant, water, is much more convenient than oil.

Return to Their Upright Position

MY LIFE HAS evolved to the point where I hear trays mentioned most often in airplane cabins as we prepare for landing. But the most important tray in my life has always been the one that sits on a ledge under the top of my carpenter's box. It holds an astonishing array of tools and miscellanea — smaller items that would take forever to find if they were mixed in with the tools in the main storage compartment deeper in the box. I've already mentioned several of these items: several pencils (carpenter's, for marking rough framing, and a regular #2 for everything else), a #2 Phillips head and a straight slot screwdriver, a small compass with a pencil stub for scribing, a bevel gauge, an adjustable wrench, a cold chisel, a plumb bob, a sharpening stone, a chalk line, spare coping saw blades, a 20-foot tape rule, and a 6-foot folding wood rule.

You might think those items would fill the space, but no. The tray is 31 inches long, divided by a crosspiece in the middle, 4½ inches wide, and a bit over an inch deep. If you pack it carefully, that's quite a lot of space. I manage to fit these items in with the rest:

Wood rasp

1. A wood rasp. Old-fashioned rasps usually had long, slightly tapered thin blades set into wood handles at one end. The one I carry is only about 6 inches long; it's thicker, flat on one side, slightly convex on the other, and has no handle. The metal surface has been machined into surfaces of varying coarseness or fineness to work on wood the way sandpaper does, scratching it down with the coarse and smoothing it with the finer grids.

Some rasps come with four different grids, two on each side, but mine has just one coarse and one fine scraping surface. In some situations, a rasp works better than a plane for the final fitting of a piece of wood.

2. A length of mason's line, for occasions when I want to establish a guideline for keeping a wall straight. If the line has been used before, it is wound around a scrap of wood, but since I don't need one very often, I might be carrying a new one in its original package.

When I discussed hammers, I mentioned that I carry a mason's hammer if the day's projects include any work with concrete block, brick, or stone. I would also then put in my box for the day two pointed mason's trowels (large and small) and a pointing or raking tool, which has a long, narrow blade curved crosswise along its entire length. After you've applied a bed of mortar and laid a course of brick or block on it, you scrape off the excess mortar extruded from the joint with one of the trowels, let the mortar set for a few minutes, then refine the joint by drawing the pointing tool along it to give it a smooth concave surface. The small pointing trowel is good for pushing mortar into any openings between sills and foundations. Sometimes I use the trowel and pointing tool together, holding the trowel next to an opening to be sealed and pushing the mortar off the trowel with the pointing tool.

3. Drill bits. My dad's toolbox always contained a bit brace for drilling by hand and, in the tray, a wooden box filled with wood-boring auger bits. I also remember him carrying a hand drill, which worked (and looked) much like an eggbeater, and an assortment of twist drill bits for it. I haven't used a bit brace since I was a child because I've grown up in the era of the power drill — and now the cordless power drill — but I have to carry the same kinds of bits in my tray, too.

   Though some people don't think of a carpenter as carrying twist drill bits since they're associated with drilling through metal rather than wood, I do carry them. They are useful for drilling pilot holes for screws or to prevent finish nails from bending or splitting the wood close to the end of a piece of hardwood trim or molding. I keep many of my twist drill bits in a spare metal bandage box rather than loose in the tray. These bits have one or more helical cutting grooves machined into the shaft and are often graded in $\frac{1}{32}$-inch increments, though some are also graded in $x/64$s. I find it useful to carry a set ranging from $\frac{1}{32}$ to $\frac{1}{4}$ inch, and I use the $\frac{1}{8}$-inch one most frequently. The most commonly used pop rivets in sheet metal work take a $\frac{1}{8}$-inch hole.

My twist drill bits don't come out of the bandage box as frequently as the brad point bits come out of the tray. I carry a set of the latter running from ⅛ to ½ inch in increments of ⅛ inch, with maybe an odd 5/16-inch one in the batch. These bits are made for wood. The shank has a helical pattern. The tip flattens out into a cutting edge similar to that of the spade bit (see below) except that it is slightly curved between the side and the sharp center point; the point cuts through wood quickly without tearing it up too much and leaves a pretty flat bottom. It's ideal for drilling holes for dowels. Brad point bits can be used in a drill press in your shop as well as in your power hand drill at a job site.

I also carry a set of spade bits (the relatively thin cylindrical shaft flattens and broadens out toward the tip into a cutting blade shaped like a spade, with a sharp point extending from the otherwise straight cutting edge). They are for drilling fairly large holes in wood — for example, holes through sheathing to attach scaffolding brackets or holes to start mortises. The bits range from ¼ inch to 1½ inches and bigger, although 1½ inches is about the largest I've ever used. They replaced the auger bits that fit bit braces.

You can't use auger bits in a power drill because they have a square end that fits the chuck of a bit brace but not a power drill. There have been times when I wanted to use an auger-type bit because of the way its threaded tip pulls itself through wood. Instead of buying new auger bits that would fit in my electric drill, I took old ones and cut the square segment off. They had to be run at low speed because they are engineered to work at the slow speed of a hand drill. For both the spade and auger bits, it is best to use an electric drill rather than a cordless model because of the extra torque needed to turn these larger bits.

Various companies grind the cutting edge of their spade bits to a slightly different profile from year to year, I find. Of all the bits I carry, the spade bits are the easiest to sharpen — on a grinding wheel or with a file. The twist drill bits can be sharpened on a grinder with a little practice, although some of them have special factory-sharpened angles that can be duplicated only on a machine; once you've dulled or damaged the factory edge, however, you can sharpen it yourself to a conventional angle. Some toolmakers provide sharpeners like pencil sharpeners for their bits.

Brad point bits and auger bits are the hardest to sharpen because there is so little cutting area to work with. But they do get damaged, most often from hitting the unseen nail. You can fix them a little with a file, but not as much as you can fix the other bits.

I remember with something approaching awe an electrician of Russian descent whom I worked with on jobs for several years. Electricians come in when the frame is complete and start to make holes in it to run their wires; they hit lots of nails. At 6 feet 9 inches, my Russian friend was tall enough to drill through ceiling joists of conventional height without having to stand on a ladder; at 320 pounds, he was strong enough to force the bit through a joist even when it was dull or damaged. He would just point the auger bit where he wanted it to go and push until he broke through.

4. I always have two metal bandage boxes in my tray. The first one, as I've just said, holds many of my bits. The other one contains bandages. (No one is perfect.)

Read the Directions, Please

I'VE NOTICED TWO things about instructions that come with tools, appliances, and materials. The first is that people often don't bother to study the sheet or manual before they plunge into action, with consequences ranging from the merely humorous to the almost disastrous. Eventually, problems drive the user back to the instructions, not just to study proper procedure but to find a way to undo a snarl thanks to the wrong way just taken.

On the other hand, I've also noticed that the instructions are frequently written as though no one expected them to be consulted. They are too brief or dense or vague or assume too much knowledge. I always take time to review the instructions in the package. Even when I'm replacing something I'm familiar with, I glance through them to see how clear they are. If everyone followed this practice, a lot of manufacturers would be besieged with demands to improve their instructions.

Free Advice

A LAWYER WHO did some work for me when I was a contractor once asked me, as a favor, to walk through the home of a potential client. This man wanted to sue his contractor for alleged damages related to a partial renovation of his house. The work had been completed two years before I saw it; on those grounds alone it was going to be difficult to sympathize with this man's sense of injury.

I attributed most of the small cracks he showed me in the joints of door frames to the way houses shift and settle over time. In one room, the homeowner pointed unhappily to an oak floor. "This is the only place I've seen on this job," I said, "where the contractor made a mistake, and, from the evidence, I'd guess he made it only after repeated callbacks." When first installed, the boards were undoubtedly tight, but they were probably put down during a humid season. Some months later, as the boards dried out from the heating in the house during the winter, they shrank slightly, and cracks opened between some of them.

I've had the same experience as a contractor. Clients have called me in December to show me cracks between boards in a floor I installed the previous summer. My advice was always the same: watch the floor until next August; if the cracks are still apparent at the height of summer's humidity, I'll come back and reinstall the floor.

Nobody ever called back in August. But in the oak floor I was looking at, the contractor — harassed, no doubt, by the homeowner — made a mistake. He caulked the cracks during the winter. When the boards swelled again the following summer, they squeezed the caulking right out of the cracks, making the homeowner doubly unhappy.

All I heard as we walked through the house, while I explained various aspects of construction, was, "I'm not hearing what I want to hear!" Finally, I said, "I'd like to know the name of your contractor because I think he does pretty good work." I don't believe my lawyer took the case, and he thanked me for helping him understand how a house breathes — expands, contracts, and shifts — with the seasons.

In Defense of Fancy

As a frontispiece to one of his excellent books on tools and carpentry, Eric Sloane quotes from a tool pamphlet published in the colonies in 1719: "The Carpenter who builds a good House to defend us from Wind and Weather, is far more serviceable than the curious Carver who employs his art to please his Fancy." I don't know whether this comparison is a universal sentiment or peculiarly American, to elevate practical crafts and housebuilding above mere carving and art — anything ornamental. There is a hint of a sneer in referring to the carver as only pleasing his fancy. "More serviceable" suggests more valuable.

In my own work, I have to say, I haven't seen this difference at all, nor do I make the comparison alleged in the old pamphlet. Just because the frame of a house will eventually be almost entirely obscured by siding, roofing, and finished interior surfaces doesn't mean that I'm indifferent to how beautifully made it is. I want the completed frame to please my fancy, too. If, as sometimes happens, I frame a wall in the morning and make a piece of furniture in the afternoon, I don't have to change mental gears. I want them both to be serviceable. I want them both to be pleasing to the eye.

Recently I've been working in Salem, Massachusetts, one of many New England towns celebrated for their early American structures. The man who contributed the most to Salem's architectural renown, Samuel McIntire, was astonishingly versatile. He was an architect and draftsman, a builder, a master carpenter, a furniture designer and maker, and a superb woodcarver. The reason his buildings are more celebrated than others of his time in Salem is that he put his fancy into every aspect of his work.

Design

A LOT OF general contractors think of themselves as designers as well as builders. No doubt, some of them are; many of them aren't. A lot of architectural designers have clever, even inventive, ideas but don't know much about construction techniques. Their suggestions may be wildly impractical or expensive to realize or both. The client stands between the two, needing to watch the cost but wanting to build something memorable. Even when you know the specific style and scale you want, a good designer will bring a sophistication to the plan that is usually beyond the capacity of his client or the contractor.

If you're not going to have the design and construction done by separate parties, it's important to search patiently until you find a builder who is thoughtful and experienced in design work. Often, builders don't spend enough time thinking about design. They get set in a pattern, and every time they run into a given situation they propose the same solution. But there are always other design possibilities.

A design generated by a contractor might err on the engineering and business side — on what's practical and feasible for him to do with little risk to his reputation, schedule, and profit margin. A designer will stress the creative aspects, but if he also knows how to build, his design will be the better for it.

This One's for You

WHEN MY FIRST book, a collection of woodworking projects, was published in 1989, I wrote two sentences for the dedication: "I dedicate this book to my father, who taught me patience, persistence, and the skills necessary for carpentry and woodworking. I now share these rewarding skills with others."

It wasn't until I had almost finished the text of this book that I saw how omnipresent my father was. I hadn't planned it, but as I was explaining a hand tool or technique, my father kept appearing as the person who had first shown it to me. I've come to regard him as my coauthor, the source of much of what I pass on to you.

In December of last year, shortly before I finished these pages, my father died, unexpectedly. We had recently agreed to get together to reminisce about some of our earliest experiences in carpentry but hadn't set a date. I had to take the initiative because my dad was as reticent as he was knowledgeable. His death surprised and saddened me, but it didn't trouble me. We were at peace with each other. There are no regrets between father and son to haunt me.

This book is not a deliberate memorial because all through the writing of it my father was alive. And, for me, he still is. Every time I pick up a tool he is as vivid to me as though I could still telephone him, invite him over to help me install more interior trim in my not-quite-finished new house, where his craftsmanship is visible everywhere I turn.

I believe the relationship between my dad's temperament and his skill was essential, not incidental. Any one of us, given just half of his patience and persistence, can become a skilled carpenter. Good tools are indispensable, but temperament is the crux.

His name was Louis Abram, but all his friends called him Louie. This one's for you, Louie.

Norm
March 1996

ACKNOWLEDGMENTS

I began this book by sitting down with my longtime producer and friend, Russ Morash. For several hours, first in Massachusetts and later in Hawaii, where we were working together, we discussed what to write about carpentry, especially the use of hand tools, that would inform and inspire people who are curious but not very experienced. Both our fathers were master carpenters, but we know that the wisdom of carpentry isn't being handed down from generation to generation as it once was. Thus the content of this book and its lessons began to evolve. Donald Cutler helped me organize the text. Pamela Hartford worked at libraries in Salem and Boston, Massachusetts, and corresponded with tool companies to gather the illustrations. Luise Erdmann went over the text thoroughly to show me where it needed more clarity or simplicity or both. I thank them all sincerely. Together we prepared my sixth book in a long and happy relationship with Little, Brown.

A Note on the Illustrations

Many of my tools have changed in their design and materials over the last hundred years, but many still bear a strong resemblance to the tools our ancestors used. Where appropriate, we have used engravings of tools from nineteenth- and early-twentieth-century catalogues.

Buck & Ryan, Ltd. (London, 1925)
Millers Falls Tools (Millers Falls, Mass., 1915)
Peter Nicholson, *The Mechanic's Companion* (Philadelphia, 1832)
Pexto Mechanic's Hand Tools (Southington, Conn., 1927)
The Sheffield Illustrated List (Pawson & Brailsford, Ltd., 1888)
Roger K. Smith, source of books and catalogues on antique tools (P.O. Box 177, Athol, Mass. 01331)
The Stanley Rule & Level Company (USA, 1870, 1879)
L. S. Starrett Company Tool Catalog (Athol, Mass., 1938)
Ward & Payne, Ltd. (Sheffield, 1911)